# A Bristol Soldier in the Second World War: Herbert Haddrell's 43 Days of Battle

# LEST WE FORGET

## *HILL 112 – NORMANDY 1944*

Morning came and rising sun
Harbinger of a day begun
In beauty – cornfields standing still
Around a gently sloping hill

Young soldiers ordered now to rise
Surveyed the scene with tired eyes,
Stretched aching bodies to the sun
For them the fateful day begun.

Their Padre, service duly said
With blessing for the way ahead,
Small wooden crosses neatly lay –
Many would not survive the day.

The "rations – up" – the order said
Each man two slices of white bread,
"White bread!" this surely must convey
The dawning of a special day.

A quiet soldier smiling said
"I'll save my slices of white bread"
And wrapped them carefully impressed
For safety, in his battle dress.

Big guns fired from fields far back
Infantry leading the attack –
New soldiers in new army-boots
Fighting seasoned Panzer troops.

Yet slowly forward – upward still
Towards the summit of the hill
They fought their way, paying the price
Of young lives, lost in sacrifice.

At long last victory! summit gained
Dark shadows closed as day light waned
And weary bodies – shattered minds
Sought comrades that they could not find.

The quiet soldier – both legs gone
Lay on a little rise – alone,
One dead hand staining brightly red
Two precious slices of white bread!

*Mary Herbert*

# A Bristol Soldier in the Second World War: Herbert Haddrell's 43 Days of Battle

Ian Haddrell

To DAVID

Best wishes

Ian Haddrell

The
History
Press

*To them that saved our heritage,*
*And cast their own away.*

Rudyard Kipling

First published 2009
Reprinted, 2019
The History Press
97 St George's Place, Cheltenham,
Gloucestershire,
www.thehistorypress.co.uk

British Library Cataloguing in Publication Data.
A catalogue record for this book is available from the British Library.

ISBN 978 0 7524 5169 5

Typesetting and origination by The History Press
Printed in Great Britain by TJ International Ltd, Padstow, Cornwall.

# Contents

# Acknowledgements

John Barry, Dr John Brenton, the *Bristol Evening Post*, the *Bristol Observer,* Bristol Record Office, the *Bristol Times and Mirror*, Laura Brouard, Sybil Cavanagh, Commonwealth War Graves Commission, David Dyer, Arthur and Pamela Haddrell, Kevin Haddrell, R.F. Hall, David Hatherell, Kenneth Hay MBE, Dr Carla Hill, Imperial War Museum, Raymond Joslin, National Archives, National Maritime Museum, National Museums of Scotland, North East Medals, David Paradise, Joanne Peacock, John Penny, Frank Porter, Tim Saunders, Stenger Historica Research Services, Ken Stovey, Paul Townsend, Revd Arthur Valle, the 43rd Wessex Association, West Lothian Health Services Archive, West Lothian Local History Library, Susan Wheeler and the *Wiltshire Gazette*.

Every effort has been made to identify copyright holders of illustrations from published materials, but I apologise to anyone overlooked in my search, or to photograph owners, should their names be omitted from the above list.

Dedicated to those who did not grow old, as those that were left grew old.

# Introduction

The first time I visited France was during the long hot summer of 1976; in fact it was the first time that I had left the shores of England. Two friends, Paul Wiltshire, Robin Butterworth, and I spent a ten-day holiday visiting Paris, and touring around parts of Brittany and Normandy in Robin's old Volkswagen Caravenette. Our journey back to the cross-channel ferry terminal at Le Havre at the end of the vacation took us along the Normandy coastline where we stopped to look at the remnants of the D-Day landings and visit the museum at Arromanches. I knew that my father had been in the Army during the Second World War and that as a member of the 4th Dorsetshire Regiment, had been badly wounded whilst serving in Normandy. However, at the time of my French holiday I had no idea when or where he had landed in France, in which area of the country he had been wounded, or what actions his battalion had participated in.

In 1982, with my wife Diane, my parents and my sister Claire, the family spent a summer holiday in Normandy, staying in a gîte in the village of Troarn, to the east of Caen. By this time, I had carried out some basic research using G.J.B. Watkins' excellent war history of the 4th Dorsets, plotting where Dad's unit had been in Normandy whilst he was serving with them, and as a result we were able to visit some of the locations and war cemeteries in the area associated with his battalion.

I returned to Normandy in the summer of 1994, this time with my parents, my wife and our twelve-year-old daughter, Georgina. The main purpose of the visit was so that my father could be presented with a commemorative medal by the Regional Council of Lower Normandy in Caen, awarded as part of the fiftieth anniversary commemoration. We again took the opportunity to visit war cemeteries where members of the 4th Dorsets had been laid to rest. This was the first occasion that I had sailed to Ouistreham, which serves as the port of the city of Caen. Sailing into the small port on a sunny summer day, with views of the now tranquil Normandy beaches, I tried to imagine what it would have been like approaching the same coastline in June 1944.

During the twenty-year period, I had been carrying out research into individuals with my surname (and variants) who had served in the Armed Forces during the First World War; the research expanded to cover all periods of military history including the Second World War. My father by then had become more involved with veterans' associations and had provided me with additional information about his brief Army career, although his memory about events in 1944 is rather vague, apart from a few specific episodes. Like many men during the battles of the Normandy campaign, my father found each day blurring into the next day. The names of towns and villages were easily forgotten – if ever known in the first place. Instead, his was a world of fields and hedgerows. However, I decided to record his limited recollections of his Army career and produce a typed version of his wartime experience as a permanent record for the family.

In 2004, sixty years after the battle for Normandy, I returned, together with my parents, to the battlefields of Normandy on a pilgrimage with a coach party of veterans, members of the 43rd Wessex Association. The organised tour retraced elements of the wartime route of the division, visiting a number of localities associated with the 4th Dorsets. Having taken the draft manuscript to France for reference, I was encouraged by fellow 'pilgrims', who had looked through it, to try and get 'the book' published.

The following narrative is reconstructed from my father's own recollections of his experience in 1944 and existing records of his battalion's actions. The accounts of men in his battalion, an application to the Ministry of Defence for information about his war service, regimental records, Official War Diaries, German unit histories, published books and museum records have all provided further sources of information.

# Chapter 1

# Growing up in Bristol

My father, Herbert Henry Haddrell, was born on 27 March 1925 at Bristol General Hospital, Guinea Street. The son of Thomas and Georgina Haddrell, he was the youngest of twelve children – six boys and six girls – born to Thomas, a dock labourer and his wife Georgina (née Lee). The family were living at No. 22 Tower Street in the parish of Temple at the time of the birth and Herbert, or Bert as he became known throughout his life, was the only child in the family to be born in hospital – his brothers and sisters all being born at home.

The Haddrell family had moved to the Temple area in the centre of Bristol in the late 1880s; the widowed Annie Haddrell, Herbert's grandmother, having brought her five children (Thomas, William, Frederick John, John, and Bessie Maud) with her from their home in the Wiltshire market town of Calne. Bert's father, Thomas, recalled that the family walked the thirty miles to Bristol with their possessions piled on a pony-drawn cart, which he had to return to Calne once the belongings had been unloaded at their new Bristol home. Annie Rogers of Horsebrook, Calne, married Tom Haddrell, a bacon curer's labourer of Oxford Road, Calne, in January 1880 at the Baptist Meeting at Calne, but by 1885 was widowed as her husband had died of typhoid fever aged twenty-eight years. A report by the Calne Hospital committee, published in the *Wiltshire Gazette* newspaper of 24 December 1885, documents that, 'Since the outbreak of the epidemic in May last twenty cases have been received into the hospital and treated. Four died in the hospital (at Mile End, Calne), viz:- Richard Beasant, Anne Taylor, Richard Edwards and Tom Haddrell.'

The 1891 census lists the Haddrell family living at No. 2 Brook's Court, Rose Street, with Annie, still a widow, supporting her family by working as a laundress. The family continued to live in the Temple area during the early part of the twentieth century, with Thomas, Annie's eldest son, taking over his mother's house by 1901, and Annie with her new husband, 'Harry' Broad, renting the adjoining house, No. 1 Brook's Court. Annie remarried on 9 December 1893 in Temple Church to Henry Broad, a thirty-seven-year-old corn porter from Winford, Somerset. When Annie Broad died in 1918, she was living at No. 60 Church Street, with her now adult sons William and John (known as Bill and Jack) living close by in No. 16 Church Street,

Annie Broad, with four of her five children; William Haddrell, John Haddrell, Frederick John Haddrell and Bessie Maud Haddrell, *c.* 1893. Her eldest son, Thomas, is missing from the photograph.

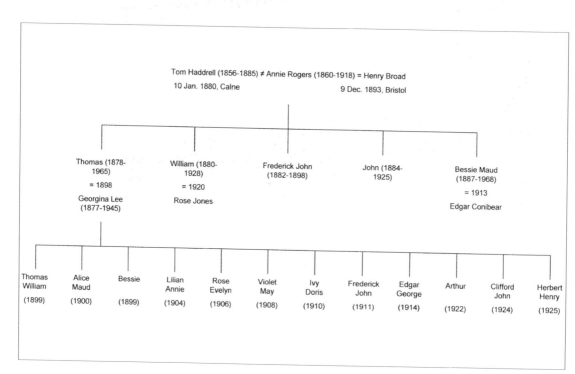

The Haddrell family tree.

until Bill married Rose Jones in 1920, at which point Jack moved in with his eldest brother Thomas, his wife Georgina and their burgeoning family.

Thomas Haddrell married Georgina Lee on Saturday 29 October 1898 at Bristol Register Office, located at the time on the ground floor of St Peter's Hospital. Thomas was employed, by Johnny Feltham, as a haulier driving a horse and cart. One of his regular haulage jobs involved transporting scenery and equipment from Temple Meads Railway Station to the Theatre Royal in King Street, and to the Princess Theatre in Park Row. It was whilst delivering to the Theatre Royal, in that era known as 'The Old Gaff', that he became acquainted with a member of the theatre's dance chorus, one Georgina Lee.

Family tradition recounts that on the morning of his wedding, Thomas was only able to take sufficient time off from work to participate in the marriage ceremony before returning to his haulage deliveries, one of which prior to the wedding had been a delivery of flour. Only able to attend the Register Office ceremony mid-deliveries, he turned up for his wedding with white dust all over his clothes.

Thomas and Georgina also resided in Church Street (at No. 19) for a period, until around 1915, after which they moved to nearby No. 22 Tower Street. The house there was on three floors, with a front room that gave access to stairs leading to the cellar, where the coal was housed. The passage from the front door led to the living room/kitchen that housed the stove. Before the gas stove was installed, cooking had been done on an open fire in the kitchen, with a very large nail above it to

The Theatre Royal, King Street, in 1890. The small covered frontage, centre of the picture, is the original entrance leading into the historic 1766 theatre. It was here that Thomas Haddrell delivered scenery and first met Georgina Lee.

Georgina Lee aged about twenty years, around 1897, in costume as a dancer at the Theatre Royal, Bristol or 'Old Gaff' as it was known at the time, a period when music hall productions were popular at the venue.

hang the cooking pots. Originally, the house was lit by oil lamps until Thomas paid to have gas installed in the property. There were two bedrooms on the first floor, 'the boys' room' and 'mother's room' – referring to the parents' bedroom; the girls were in the bedroom on the second floor. The yard at the rear of the house was a stone paved area where fowls, pigeons, rabbits and ducks were kept. Thomas wouldn't kill the animals himself, so he would ask their next door neighbour, Jack Whiting, to slaughter the animals for him. The house had a shared water supply and shared toilet which, together with the washroom, were at the bottom of the yard. The washroom housed a tin bath where the children were washed and scrubbed by Georgina, and then wrapped in a towel and made to run across the yard to the house to warm in front of the fire. The toilet had to be flushed with buckets of water, taking great care not to pour water over the seat. When it was dark, illumination for the toilet was provided by a single candle brought from the house. Sometimes there were rats in the rafters of the toilet, which came into the property from the stables in Avon Street, beyond the yard. Behind the rear of the house there was a chapel and 'Gran' Broad would sing along with the hymns being sung at the Sunday service.

Fred and Ivy Haddrell had many memories of their childhood in the Temple area. There were two pubs in Rose Street, the Apple Tree and the Cherry Tree, and a Jewish burial ground nearby. Welsh cockle girls lodged in Church Street and a special treat was a ½d glass of ice cream from an Italian ice cream seller who came round with his cart on Sundays. Bert's sister Ivy recalled buying onions for 1d to

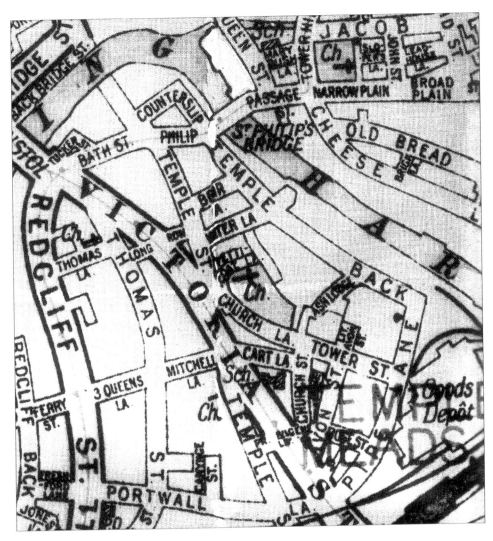

Street plan of the Temple area of Bristol, 1925.

make onion broth and eating 'muggets' and cows udders. 'The Plankard family lived on the corner and mother did washing for them'. Fred was awarded a Foundation Scholarship at Temple Colston School in Victoria Street, a school originally founded by Edward Colston, the merchant and philanthropist born in Temple parish. Fred remembered the Temple Institute in Tower Street that offered, amongst other things, billiards, a skittle alley and Bible classes on Sunday afternoons. There were many stables in the area, including the Great Western Railway (GWR) stables at the top of Tower Street; Pickfords, who kept their animals and carts in Pipe Lane; and J.C. Walls in Ash Lodge.

Shortly after Bert's birth in 1925, Thomas moved his family from the Temple area to Knowle Park in Bristol, being re-housed in a house erected by the GWR as alternative accommodation for the tenants of old property being demolished at Temple in the course of clearing ground for the new GWR goods yard. The Labouring Classes Dwelling Act provided that, before tenants could be disturbed, suitable alternative accommodation had to be found for them. The railway company built a block of fifty properties – twenty-six parlour type and twenty-four non-parlour type – situated at Greenleaze Road, Kingshill Road and Queensdale Road, and it was to No. 68 Kingshill Road that the family eventually moved. Difficulties arose because the new properties were of a type and rental not suited to some of the people who occupied the old property. Family tradition has it that Thomas was reluctant to move out of the Temple area and that the Haddrells were one of the last families to leave because of his obstinacy.

Now working as a labourer at Bristol docks, Thomas Haddrell had to report each day to the docks office to 'sign on' to see if he was required for work. If not wanted that day he would return home; the consequence of 'nothing about today' was, of course, no pay. When old enough, Thomas's eldest sons were required to take their father's meals to him at the docks and if he began work early, they too would have an early start taking his breakfast to him. A family tradition is that Thomas and a man named Harry Rogers were among the first to join their trade union at the same time as Ernest Bevin, later a Labour leader, politician and statesman. Bevin worked as a lorry driver in Bristol, where he joined the Bristol Socialist Society. In 1910 he became secretary of the Bristol branch of the Dockers' Union, and in 1914 he became a national organiser for the union.

The Haddrell family were not affluent and didn't have a lot, but despite having difficulty in managing financially, Georgina ensured that the children didn't 'go short'. Despite being the youngest of the family, Bert didn't consider that he was spoilt as a child, but as his numerous brothers and sisters tended to look after him that he had a somewhat 'sheltered childhood'. His eldest brother, Tom, twenty-six years older, did tend to boss the younger children about, even though, being married, he

Photograph from the *Bristol Times and Mirror*, dated 4 March 1925, showing the GWR goods yard and behind the wall, the area around Rose Street and Tower Street.

no longer lived at the family home. His brother Fred, fifteen years older than Bert, ensured that he carried out his regular little jobs at home, such as tidying up around the house. As youngsters, the Haddrell children were taught simple cooking skills by their mother and Bert was able to make toast, porridge, and fry eggs and bacon, initially having to stand on a chair to be able to reach the cooker.

Thomas had a reputation for spending most of his leisure hours in public houses rather than at home with the family. However, despite being 'the worse for wear' following his many evenings spent in local hostelries, Bert remembers his father as always being clean and smart, 'happy and never violent', returning home with his hat perched on the back of his head. On an extremely rare occasion, 'Mother got drunk at Christmas and my brother Fred and sister Ivy cooked dinner, served up the chicken and had to put the presents in the stockings'. Thomas enforced a curfew on his children by locking the front door of the house at the allotted time. On one occasion Fred, who had been out with his pals Cliff Tanner and Bill Sage, arrived home late without his front door key, found the door bolted and had to call out to his father for a key to get in. Thomas threw down a front-door key from his upstairs bedroom, deliberately tossing it into the grass in the front garden, rather than to Fred, so that he had to search on his hands and knees in the dark.

Bert had a happy childhood in Knowle and remembers going to see the first film at the Gaiety Cinema, on the corner of Crossways Road and Wells Road, Knowle, a five-minute walk from his house. When the cinema opened in 1933, with Jessie Matthews in the film *The Good Companions*, it was described as 'a new super-cinema for a growing suburb'.

Cliff Haddrell, Arthur Haddrell and Bert Haddrell, with their sister's dog Jack, in the rear garden of their home at 68 Kingshill Road, Knowle Park, *c.* 1929.

Bert has fond childhood memories of his time spent at the local Sunday school in Upper Knowle Methodist Church hall:

> We had a wonderful Sunday school superintendant, Mr Smith, and I worshipped the ground that he walked on. When he wanted a reading done he would ask me and after I had finished he would say, 'Well done Herbert', which I was very pleased about.

The highlight of the whole year was the Sunday school anniversary and the accompanying concert, which required regular practice attendance:

> We had Madam Ivy Wallace, a professional singer, to teach us and I was fascinated by her conducting because for rehearsals she had a little wooden baton, but when it was the actual anniversary she used a black one with a silver top. I thought this was lovely. I used to stand in the front and she used to say to me, 'Herbert, smile'.

Another high spot in the Sunday school calendar was the annual outing to the seaside:

> It was just a lovely gathering really, something that you looked forward to – a treat – because we didn't really go many places in those days. In my family we never went on holiday, so the Sunday school outing was a special treat. It was an event you see, one of the events of the year.

Bert joined the local Cub pack and the 252nd Scout group at Upper Knowle Methodist Church, enjoying the fellowship of the other boys and the numerous activities that scouting provided. He particularly enjoyed camping, remembering one occasion when, as a scout, he went to Tickenham, a village to the south of Bristol, on a Cub camp to help the leaders. The church hall was also the venue for concerts and plays which Bert participated in, until the declaration of war in 1939 when all such activities ceased. At the time he was rehearsing the play *Toad of Toad Hall* in which he played the part of 'Ratty'. However, the production was cancelled as the hall was requisitioned for use as a mortuary. He attended Knowle Park Infants School, Knowle Park Junior School and Merrywood Grammar School for Boys, one of the earliest publicly-funded schools in Bristol. At junior school, Bert recalls being particularly 'miffed about being caned' as he felt that he had been unfairly treated. He was sent to the headmistress, Mrs Kent, for a misdemeanour that had occurred in the playground at lunchtime and was told to wait outside her door for her return. She returned to her office after lessons had already started and promptly caned Bert for being late for his lesson. Having taken and passed a grammar school entrance exam, Bert won a scholarship, initially to St George Grammar School, but this was revised to Merrywood Grammar School for Boys, which was initially located in Bedminster; the school later moved to Novers Hill, Knowle whilst Bert was still a pupil. The family received a grant to help pay for Bert's schoolbooks which had to be paid for by the pupil at that time. As a student at secondary school, Bert was particularly interested in Art, French and English, enjoying reading, but, by his own admission, wasn't particularly good at Maths. 'I was no good at sport and would get out of doing it if possible.'

Technical skills were also something that Bert wasn't particularly adept at, as his woodwork master Mr 'Taper' Wood remarked that he couldn't even plane a piece of wood – one of the subject's basic skills.

Bert's father, Thomas, took him away from school at the age of fourteen as he said that he couldn't afford to keep him there and that he needed to go out and get a job. Thomas showed no real interest in his son's future career plans and left any decisions to his wife, Georgina. On leaving school in 1939, Bert wrote for a job to a local printing firm, Burleighs Ltd, in Lewins Mead, owned by members of the Corrigan family. Being successful in his application he joined the company as a reader's assistant, which involved reading galley proofs out loud to a senior reader who would then make the necessary corrections – effectively proof-reading. A galley proof is a printout of a document in which the margins are especially large. The idea is that one can read over what has been printed and have room for writing comments. He recalls being admonished on a number of occasions by John Windows, one of the senior readers, being told to 'cut out the histrionics' as he didn't require a dramatic performance whilst trying to correct the text. Wages were approximately 10s a week,

MERRYWOOD SECONDARY SCHOOL, BRISTOL, OCT., 1936.

Merrywood Grammar School for Boys, October 1936. Bert, aged eleven years, is the pupil on the far right of the back row. The schoolmaster is Mr Nicholson.

which Bert handed over to his mother in totality; she then gave him money for bus fares, dinner and a half-crown (2s 6d) pocket money each week. Bert didn't stay long at his first job and found employment next as an office boy at a financier's office, F.G. Price Ltd, High Street, Bristol – in reality money lenders. At times he was sent out on his own to collect money from customers and then bring it back to the office; something he didn't like doing at a young age. Sometimes Bert would arrive home late from work, because the air-raid sirens had sounded and as the buses then stopped running, he would have to get off and walk the remainder of the way to Knowle. His mother was always very worried when this happened even though there were no actual German air-raids over Bristol at the time.

On Sunday 3 September 1939, at a little after 11 a.m., Bert listened on the radio at his sister Alice's house in Hanham, where she lived with her husband Art Heales, to the announcement by Prime Minister Neville Chamberlain that Britain was at war with Germany, but at the time didn't realise the full implication of what was being said and the impact that it would have on his life. This was how the war began for Bert and for millions of other families throughout Great Britain. Few can have foreseen on that sunny September morning what lay ahead and the great transformations that would occur in their lives. Certainly, as a schoolboy of fourteen, Bert did not anticipate that before the war was over he would be in the Army on the Continent.

Once the war started, Bert undertook voluntary work during the evening in a local hall with a group of young fellows, taking apart gas masks and putting the separated parts in boxes, although he no longer recalls the purpose of this exercise. Everyone had been issued with a gas mask by the time of the Munich crisis in September 1938. For many people the sensation of clammy breathlessness and smell of rubber and disinfectant they experienced when donning the mask was the first intimation of the approaching war; the distribution of the masks by thousands of volunteers was their introduction to the communal effort which was to characterise the Home Front during the war years. Gas masks came in an amazing array of shapes and sizes. Newborn babies had a ghastly one-piece mask that covered the whole body. The baby was strapped into a small air-tight chamber into which filtered air was pumped by means of a hand bellows. It is claimed that most babies fell soundly asleep when placed in these helmets (probably close to suffocation), but fortunately these helmets were never needed, apart from for a few publicity photos. Bert also helped at home with the blackout precautions for the house, sticking adhesive tape on the window panes to stop glass splinters if they were shattered, and helping put up blackout curtains to ensure no light from the room could be seen outside that might guide German bombers. During the war, everyone had to cover their windows and doors at night (before sunset) with heavy blackout curtains, cardboard or paint. Wardens would patrol, checking up on any sources of light and if light was visible from outside, the householder could be fined.

In October 1940, aged fifteen years, Bert joined H.J. Packer & Co. Ltd, chocolate manufacturers, as a general office boy working in Carlyle Road, Greenbank, Bristol, where both the offices and factory were located. He was to remain with the company under its various guises of Carsons, Cavenham Confectionery, Famous Names, and Elizabeth Shaw, for forty-seven and a half years. Travelling by bus to work from Knowle, Bert remembers the wonderful smell of chocolate as he approached the factory along Co-operation Road on his first day at work, and that one had to sign in before 9 a.m. when a red line was drawn across the book, and your signature would have to be written below the line, indicating that you were late for work. Duties in his first job at Packers included dealing with the post, ensuring that it was franked or correctly stamped; answering the only telephone that the company possessed, situated near the post desk, and dealing with the calls; compiling the 'cigarette list' which necessitated finding out what cigarettes the office staff wanted to buy, collecting their money, and then going to purchase them from a chap called Ray Wade who worked in the factory office; daily taking round the handwritten menu to staff, including the directors, to establish what they wanted for lunch that day before taking their selections to Mrs Cooper in the canteen – who always gave Bert the first piece of bread pudding that she made every Tuesday; and going to Culliford's Post Office, which stood on the corner of Co-operation Road and Camelford Road, to buy National Insurance stamps. For many decades, employee and employer contributions were collected by the sale (to employers) of insurance stamps at Post Offices. The employer then affixed the stamps to contribution cards weekly. Mrs Tavener provided Bert with a list of stamps to buy and the funds to do so. Before long, Bert was promoted to the sales ledger section of the company, which was responsible for the inputting of all externally raised invoices and credit notes, despite, by his own admission, being 'no good at Maths at school'. However, he soon mastered the necessary skills for the job and by the time he left Packers to

The factory of H.J. Packer's, chocolate manufacturer, Greenbank, Bristol. Bert spent forty-seven and a half years – from 1940 to 1988 – working in the office block in the bottom right of the picture.

join the Army he had moved to the sales office, working in a team of two; himself and his boss Roger Cole.

He also worked a fire-watching shift at Packers in case incendiary bombs were dropped on the factory. Incendiary bombs, also known as firebombs, were used as an effective bombing weapon in the Second World War. The large bomb casing was filled with small sticks of incendiaries (bomblets) and designed to open at altitude, scattering the bomblets in order to cover a wide area. An explosive charge would then ignite the incendiary material, often starting a raging fire. The fire would burn at extreme temperatures that could destroy most buildings made of wood or other combustible materials. Dropped by the Luftwaffe in their thousands, the 1kg incendiary bomb posed a tremendous problem for fire-fighters. Having received no training, Bert was issued with a stirrup pump as the only measure to deal with any fires. Stirrup pumps were issued to thousands of householders at the outbreak of the war as a means of controlling the effects of incendiary bomb attacks. However, in practice it was soon discovered that the simple expedient of throwing a bucket of water over the bomb had quicker results. Fortunately for him, no incendiaries dropped on the chocolate factory when he was on duty.

# Chapter 2

# The War Comes to Knowle

The Luftwaffe orders for the night of Sunday 24 November 1940 were for the first major attack on *Bruder*, the German code name for Bristol, but as there had been a good deal of fog over Northern France earlier in the day, and a chance that it might return, it was decided operations should be completed by midnight. A total of 148 aircraft – using three principal types of bomber, the Dornier Do 17, the Heinkel He 111 and the Junkers Ju 88, all twin-engined aircraft – were ordered to the city, 135 of which claimed to have attacked between 1830 and 2300 hrs with 156.25 tonnes of H.E.'s (High Explosives), 4.75 tonnes of Oil Bombs and 12,500lbs of Incendiary Bombs. The concentration point was centred on the harbour and industrial plants on both sides of the city docks, with the intention of 'eliminating Bristol as an importing port supplying much of the Midlands and South of England'. The aircraft involved in this operation were drawn from I/KG 1, III/KG 26, and III/KG 27; I, II and III/KG 51; Stab, I, II and III/KG 55; KGr.100, KGr.606, and LG 1.

For the Germans it was a successful night and only two aircraft failed to return, a Heinkel of II/KG 55 shot down off Portsmouth by anti-aircraft fire and a Dornier from KGr.606 which crashed near Plymouth, as a result of which four crewmen were killed and a further four made prisoner, including one who was injured. The general impression given by participating airmen was that results were similar to those achieved at Birmingham and Coventry. The attack, however, resulted in the death of 200 Bristolians, and injuries to a further 8,909. It had concentrated on the central area, with further damage occurring in Clifton, Temple, Knowle, Barton Hill and Eastville, but greatest destruction took place in the heart of the city from Broad Quay to Old Market, whilst the churches of St James' Barton and St Philip's suffered severely. Exceedingly large calibre bombs were reported as having fallen at Eastville, Speedwell, Temple and Totterdown, while for the greater part of the night the city was blazing furiously and many well-known buildings were totally destroyed and others gravely damaged.

The Haddrell family residence, No. 68 Kingshill Road, Knowle, became one of the 10,000 homes damaged by the first major air-raid attack on Bristol. Another casualty of that first Bristol Blitz was Temple Church; gutted by incendiary bombs but its leaning tower remained standing. Sappers thought that German bombs were the

Temple Church prior to November 1940 showing the extent to which the church tower leaned. The narrow streets in the vicinity of the church were home to the Haddrell family from the late nineteenth century to 1925.

St Peter's Hospital was located in Peter Street, between St Peter's Church and the Floating Harbour. The Register Office occupied part of the ground floor and it was here that Thomas Haddrell married Georgina Lee on 29 October 1898. The building was destroyed during the Blitz on 24 November 1940.

cause and that the tower should be hauled down. They had to be persuaded that the leaning was not the result of enemy action, but that it had leaned 5ft off perpendicular since 1460. Temple Church, or more correctly Holy Cross, was built on the site of the oval church of the Knights Templar.

A number of Bert's family were married in Temple Church. His grandmother, Ann Haddrell, remarried there in 1893 to Henry Broad. His uncle, Bill (William) Haddrell, married Rose Jones in 1920, and two sisters, Bess and Alice, were also married in the church. From 1898 the parish registers record the baptisms of Thomas and Georgina's twelve children, Bert included, but these registers were either destroyed or severely damaged as a result of the destruction of the church during the Blitz. St Peter's Hospital, one of the city's finest Tudor houses, and at the time housing the register office for births, marriages and deaths, was also destroyed. Thomas Haddrell and Georgina Lee, Bert's father and mother, were married there in October 1898.

Thomas Haddrell had, for reasons best known to himself, refused to have an air-raid shelter installed in his house. Consequently, Georgina, Bert, Fred and Cliff used the Anderson shelter in their next door neighbours', the Sanders family, garden, whilst Thomas normally remained inside No. 68 during enemy raids. At the time of the raid on the evening of 24 November, Cliff was attending church:

We knew there was a chance it might be Bristol's turn. Coventry and other cities had just had blitzes, so we suspected it might be us next time. I was fifteen – I'd left school at fourteen – and was the youngest of twelve children, six boys and six girls. I worked as an office boy for the chocolate-makers H.J. Packer in Greenbank. Father was a docker and mother a housewife and there were three boys still living at home in Kingshill Road in Knowle Park.

It had been a pretty usual sort of Sunday with church and Sunday school and a quiet afternoon. We had our tea at five o'clock – bread and butter and tinned fruit, we always had tinned fruit on Sundays – and we waited for my brother Fred to come home from work at the BAC [Bristol Aeroplane Company]. His tea was laid out for him.

After he got back, he washed and when he looked out of the window, he saw flares lighting up the sky like daylight. He'd been through the big raid on Filton a couple of months before and he said, 'It looks like trouble. Come on.' We didn't have our own shelter. Father wouldn't have one. I don't know why. Parents didn't discuss things like that with children in those days. You were seen and not heard.

In earlier raids, Mother and I went to a neighbour's shelter but my brother said the best thing was to make our way to the nearest public shelter which was by the shops at the top of Red Lion Hill. There was my mother, father, brother and myself, but before we could get out of the house all hell let loose when the bombs started falling. We took shelter under the stairs whilst the high explosives and the incendiary bombs were falling all around. The windows were all blown in and we just crouched there for what seemed an eternity. At last there was a lull in the bombing and my brother said he thought that we ought to try to make it to the public shelter.

We put on our outdoor clothes and were standing behind the front door waiting for my father to lace up his boots, which took a little while. We went on at him, 'Come on,

Dad, hurry up', but he took his time. That delay probably saved our lives because, as we were trying to get him to hurry up, a bomb fell in the road just outside the house. The blast threw us all backwards; the door blew in and fell down on my mother. If Dad hadn't been so slow, we would have been killed. We found out afterwards that a neighbour who was outside looking for his dog was blown to bits.

We crouched under the stairs again, covered in broken glass and debris, for what seemed like an eternity until there was another lull. Then we ventured forth. It took ages to get there. Mother suffered badly with her legs and we didn't know then that she'd been injured with a big splinter from the door. She kept saying, 'Leave me to die, leave me', but we wouldn't and my brother and I sort of dragged her along. At last we got there. It took us half an hour to do what would have been a ten minute walk for most people.

I don't think I was frightened. There was too much going on to be frightened. It was when you had to sit there and listen to the bombs coming and thinking that the next one might have your number on it that you were frightened, not when you were busy.

We spent the rest of the night in the shelter, staying there till dawn. When we got out, it was an incredible sight, mess everywhere. When we got back to our home the roof was damaged, door gone, windows all smashed in. We'd lost most of our possessions but I'll never forget seeing my brother's tea still on the table, the tinned fruit ruined.

We never went back to the house. They repaired it later but father just wouldn't return. We went to stay with a brother at Bedminster and later we went to my sister's house in Hanham because it was a bit out of town.

I heard all about the damage in the city but didn't go down there for some time. Then when I did I just felt very, very sad for all we'd lost. What really upset me was losing the old Dutch House. As a little lad I'd been taken down to the old Wine Street/Castle Street shopping area and I was fascinated by the Dutch House…it always made me think of something out of a fairy tale. It was so sad what had happened to the old heart of the city. There had been so many lovely old shops there and it was so popular. But it was all gone.

I've been back to Kingshill Road since then. I had lots of friends there and many memories. The house is still there and I always remember that last night we had there.

Georgina went to hospital the next day as she was distressed, complaining that her arm was causing her pain. It was discovered that she had a large wooden splinter embedded in her arm that had to be removed by the medical staff. As the house in Kingshill Road was now uninhabitable following the bomb damage, the family went to stay with Tom Haddrell, Bert's eldest brother, in Bedminster and afterwards spent some time with his eldest sister, Alice, and her husband, Art Heales, at Hanham. Following the raid, the house in Kingshill Road was still in a sound condition, despite the windows and doors having been blown in, with the only casualties being the budgerigars that Fred bred for sale at 2s 6d, who had disappeared from their aviary in the back garden following the bomb blast. After the property was repaired, the railway company offered to re-house the family there, but Thomas refused to move back in, the Haddrells eventually settling at No. 1 Victoria Avenue, Redfield, in a house that they rented from Art Heales.

The seventeenth-century six-storey timber-framed 'Dutch House' stood on the corner of Wine Street and High Street in central Bristol. On Sunday 24 November 1940 Bristol suffered its worst air-raid of the Second World War. Much of the historic area around High Street was destroyed and the 'Dutch House' was gutted by fire. The remaining shell was pulled down.

Three of Bert's five brothers served in the Armed Forces during the Second World War. Edgar George Haddrell emigrated to Queensland, Australia, in the 1930s under a government emigration scheme, the 'Big Brother Movement', a plan aimed to bring to the country youths from Great Britain to work on farms or in the Australian outback, in line with the government maxim on maintaining a stable level of population. On his arrival in Australia, Edgar was initially employed on a sheep station, later finding work as a gardener and part-time fireman in Townsville, Queensland, a coastal town with a population of 30,000 inhabitants in 1936. Jilted by his girlfriend, he enlisted in the Australian Army on 21 October 1939 at Townsville, joining the 2/12th Australian Infantry Battalion, arriving in the United Kingdom with his unit on 17 June 1940.

Edgar visited his mother and family at Kingshill Road in November 1940, whilst stationed at Colchester, prior to embarking for North Africa. He requested leave from his officer, but when this was refused he went AWOL (absent without leave) from his unit from 0630 hrs on 8 November to 2200 hrs on 11 November, for which he forfeited four days pay and was fined 30s. Edgar had come to Bristol with a pal from the Australian forces and when Bert first saw the pair of them together mistook this friend for Edgar, who had left home when Bert was young and had no real recollection of his brother.

A German bomb landed in the road outside of No. 68 Kingshill Road on Sunday 24 November 1940, causing the front door to be blown in on top of Georgina Haddrell, pictured here pre-war.

Thomas Haddrell stood by the front gate of his home, No. 68 Kingshill Road. Lacing his boots during the air-raid probably saved his family's lives. A pre-war photograph as there are no bomb blast precautions on the windows.

Edgar George Haddrell, born 1914, emigrated to Queensland, Australia, in the 1930s under a government emigration scheme, the 'Big Brother Movement'. He enlisted in the Australian Army in 1939 and was killed 5 August 1941 during the siege of Tobruk.

Edgar Haddrell, Georgina Haddrell, and the unknown Australian serviceman, who Bert mistook for Edgar when he first encountered the two 'diggers'.

Photograph taken during the visit of Edgar Haddrell to the family home in Bristol in early November 1940. From left to right, back row: Tom Haddrell, Edgar Haddrell, unknown, Arthur Haddrell. Front row: Cliff Haddrell, Bert Haddrell.

This short visit to the family home in Bristol was the first time that Edgar had seen any members of his family since he had departed for Australia ten years earlier – he never saw them again. Edgar Haddrell was wounded in the right thumb by gunshot during the night of 3/4 May 1941 whilst Australian forces were under siege in the Mediterranean seaport of Tobruk, Libya. Admitted to the 4th Australian General Hospital in the town, he rejoined his unit on 6 May. He was killed on 5 August 1941 whilst Tobruk was still besieged by German and Italian forces and is buried in Tobruk War Cemetery.

Arthur Haddrell enlisted on 30 April 1942, carrying out his basic infantry training with the Royal Sussex Regiment at Chichester before being transferred to the Royal Corps of Signals and posted to 3rd Holding Battalion on 25 June 1942. The Royal Signals was one of the combat support arms of the British Army responsible for installing, maintaining and operating all types of telecommunications equipment and information systems. Further tuition at Huddersfield ensued before completing his signals training at Catterick Camp, the large signals depot in Yorkshire. Arthur saw service as a dispatch rider and driver, transporting large mail bags and orders from one signals station to another in Palestine and Syria, and with the 8th Army in the Middle East. Other duties

The original cross on the grave of Private QX.2022 Edgar George Haddrell in Tobruk War Cemetery, Libya (Plot 4, Row Q, Grave 4), taken in 1943. Photograph supplied by Directorate of Graves Registration, Victoria Barracks, Melbourne.

involved driving 15cwt lorries, transporting officers and Army personnel between signals units. His postings included the 4th Line of Communications Signals, Tobruk District Signals, Benghazi District Signals and Alexandria Signals. On one occasion his unit were issued with civilian clothes as they prepared to go into neutral Turkey, where it was believed the Germans were operating. As the Signals reached the border heading for Adana, the fourth largest city in Turkey, the order came for them to abandon the mission and return. Shortly before demobilization, Arthur's unit was sent to Italy for a short period whilst part of the Central Mediterranean Force. He was released to the Territorial Army Reserve on 16 March 1947, being discharged from Reserve Liability in 1959.

Whilst stationed at Tobruk, Arthur's signals' office was located near to the cemetery incorporating the burial ground used during the siege of Tobruk. During some spare time he visited the cemetery, seven kilometres inland on the El Adem-Alexandria road, and whilst wandering around came upon his brother's grave. Arthur knew that Edgar had been killed earlier in the war but had no indication as to where he had been buried. Forbidden to carry cameras whilst on active service, Arthur asked an officer to take a picture of the grave, which he then sent to his mother in Bristol without being able to provide her with any details of its location, because of military

Driver 14212757 Arthur Haddrell taken in either Cairo or Alexandria, Egypt. Notification of awards had come through, but medals were not issued until after the war. An Egyptian photography shop had the unofficial 8th Army ribbons made up for servicemen to have souvenir pictures taken.

censorship. Subsequently the Australian Commonwealth War Graves Commission sent Georgina details of her son's last resting place, from which she was able to deduce where Arthur had been stationed.

On another occasion whilst in Egypt, probably in 1943, Arthur met his brother Cliff whose ship HMS *Active* had come into the port of Alexandria. The ship had been patrolling the Mediterranean, around the island of Rhodes, and docked for re-fuelling. Once ashore, Cliff telephoned the Signals Office in Alexandria to ask if a message could be passed to his brother, whose exact whereabouts he was uncertain of, that he was in Alexandria and wanted to meet him. The local Signals Office conveyed the message to Arthur's unit, somewhere further up the desert, where an officer granted him three days leave to visit Cliff, recommending the Hotel Cecil to stay in whilst in the city. Arthur and Cliff spent their time together exploring Alexandria, with Arthur being treated to a visit on board HMS *Active* where he received the traditional tot of navy rum.

Clifford John Haddrell, at the time employed as a dispatch rider, joined the Royal Navy in 1942, reporting on 11 November at HMS *Raleigh*, a training establishment for Ordinary Seaman, on the outskirts of Torpoint, Cornwall. Having completed the first phase of naval training, he was assigned to HMS *Drake*, a shore establishment at HMNB (His Majesty's Naval Base) Devonport, 20 January 1943. He joined his first seagoing ship, HMS *Active*, an A-class destroyer that took part in the sinking of four enemy submarines during the war, on 26 March. During the later part of the war the ship served as convoy escort, mainly between Great Britain and Sierra Leone, after receiving increased anti-aircraft and anti-submarine armament. On 23 May 1943, together with the frigate HMS *Ness*, HMS *Active* sank the Italian submarine *Leonardo da Vinci* – which was returning from a successful patrol off South Africa – north-east of the Azores. On 1 November 1943, with other British naval ships, HMS *Active* carried out depth-charge attacks on the German submarine *U-340* close to Tangier, which was scuttled the following day. HMS *Active* had the distinction of serving in many areas during the Second World War and was one of very few destroyers built before 1939 to survive the war without major damage.

Ten months after joining HMS *Active*, on 11 November 1943, Cliff was promoted to the rank of Able Seaman, the rank he retained until leaving the service in 1946. He left his ship on 21 June 1945, having spent the month of May on HMS *Cormorant*, a floating hulk, once an old warship, used as a Base Depot Ship at Gibraltar. Returning to England, Cliff spent the final year of his naval career at HMS *Drake* and HMS *Defiance*, shore establishments in Devonport, Plymouth. He was released to shore in Class A on 20 June 1946. Class A meant that he was fit and could be called up again quickly, should the need arise.

The eldest brother, Thomas William Haddrell, served in France and Belgium as a Lewis Gunner, with the 15th Battalion, the Hampshire Regiment during the later stages of the Great War. He had been wounded by gunshot in October 1918 and was recovering in the 1st Birmingham War Hospital, Rednal, when the Armistice was signed on 11 November. He was forty-one years old when war broke out again.

The remaining brother, Frederick John Haddrell, was employed by the BAC (Bristol Aeroplane Company) at Filton on the outskirts of Bristol and was not called up because his job, of a secretive nature, was classified as a reserved occupation and he was thus exempt from military conscription. However, as well as his important, regular full-time daytime work, he also enlisted in one of the Gloucestershire (City of Bristol) Battalions of the Home Guard. The Home Guard (initially Local Defence

Clifford John Haddrell served on HMS *Active* between 26 March 1943 and 21 June 1945. During the war all naval hatbands were plain, with no ship's name attached.

Thomas Haddrell served with the 15th Battalion, Hampshire Regiment during the First World War as a Lewis Gunner, identified by the insignia on his left sleeve. The crossed rifles signify that he was a marksman. He was wounded by gunshot during the later stages of 1918, being hospitalized in the 1st Birmingham War Hospital, Rednal.

Volunteers or LDV) was a defence organisation active in the United Kingdom during the Second World War which acted as a secondary defence force in case of invasion by the forces of Nazi Germany, guarding the coastal areas of Britain and other important places such as factories and explosives stores.

On the evening of 14 May 1940, the Secretary of State for War, Anthony Eden, gave a radio broadcast announcing the formation of the Local Defence Volunteers and called for volunteers to join the force. In the radio announcement, Eden called on men between the ages of seventeen and sixty-five in Britain, who were not in military service but wished to defend their country against an invasion, to enroll in the LDV at their local police station. The announcement was met with a great deal of enthusiasm on the part of the population, with 250,000 volunteers attempting to sign up in the first seven days; by July this number would increase to 1.5 million. Even once the threat of invasion had passed, the Home Guard remained in existence, manning guard posts and performing other duties to free regular troops for duties overseas. In 1942 the National

Service Act allowed for compulsory enrolment where units were below strength. At this time, the lowest rank within the Home Guard, 'volunteer', was renamed to 'private' to match the regular Army usage. However, following the successful invasion of France and the drive towards Germany by Allied armies, the Home Guard were formally stood down on 3 December 1944 and finally disbanded on 31 December 1945.

A Certificate of Proficiency dated 11 September 1944 records that Fred, whilst serving in 101 Battery, the 17th Regiment Home Guard, qualified in the Proficiency Badge tests for 'Z' AA Battery work. From April 1942, Home Guard anti-aircraft units were formed and by 1944 these units had taken over many anti-aircraft batteries, operating artillery from the light to heavy guns and also the semi-secret rocket batteries (also known as 'Z' Batteries). A 'Z' Battery consisted of sixty-four projectors (rocket launchers), each one firing two rounds for a total of 128 rounds per salvo. Each projector could fire two 3in anti-aircraft rockets, having a maximum altitude of 19,000ft and a ground range of 10,000yds (5.7 miles). The heavy finned rockets were about 6ft long and each had an adjustable nose fuse to be set to explode the warhead at the correct altitude. Two men manned each projector. The commands for altitude, bearing, elevation, loading, etc. came over a sound-powered intercom from the operations room to a headphone worn by No.1, who relayed the orders to No.2. Each man set a fuse, No.2 loaded the rockets onto their guide rails and pulled them down onto the electrical firing pins and then set the elevation wheel. The firing pins were connected via safety switches to a firing handle and a 6 volt dry battery. No.1 set the bearing and reported 'Charlie 5 ready'; on the command 'Fire', he depressed the firing handle.

Fred's unit, 101 Rocket Battery (Easton in Gordano) affiliated to the 9th Battalion Home Guard based in the Horfield area, spent time guarding Portishead, a North Somerset coastal village on the Bristol Channel, twelve miles from Bristol. It was here that he went at weekends and when not working at the aircraft factory at Filton, or 'drome' (aerodrome) as he referred to it. As well as a series of anti-aircraft batteries in the area, Portishead was also home to a radio station that provided world-wide maritime communications and long-range aeronautical communications from 1928 until 2000. The station played a vital role during the Second World War in maintaining communications with the British Merchant Navy and with patrol aircraft in the North Atlantic. During the war, all communications with ships were one-way in order to avoid revealing the ships' locations to the enemy. Prior to joining the local Home Guard, Fred had been a member of the Central Division of the Bristol Street Fire Guard Organisation.

# Chapter 3

# Call Up

On 27 April 1939, Parliament passed the Military Training Act. This act introduced conscription for men aged twenty and twenty-one who were now required to undertake six months military training. On the outbreak of the Second World War, Parliament passed the National Service (Armed Forces) Act, under which all men between eighteen and forty-one were made liable for conscription. It was also announced that single men were called up before married men. The registration of all men in each age group in turn began on 21 October for those aged twenty to twenty-three. By May 1940, registration had extended only as far as men aged twenty-seven and did not reach those aged forty until June 1941.

By the end of 1939 over 1.5 million men had been recruited into the Armed Forces. Of these, 1,128,000 joined the British Army and the remainder were equally divided between the Royal Navy and the Royal Air Force. For thousands of young men conscripted into the three services, it was their first time away from home and they all coped with it in their own way. At eighteen years of age, young men had to register for service and had a choice; if they were doing an apprenticeship or any sort of training for a career, they could opt to defer their service until they were twenty-one.

The easiest way to avoid conscription was to ignore the summons to register for National Service. As a result of a shortage of people to enforce attendance, this method of avoiding joining the Armed Forces was highly effective. Another method was to hire a man who had already failed his medical to impersonate you in front of the medical board. There was also a good market in buying forged medical discharge certificates.

Provision was made in the legislation for people to object to military service on moral grounds. Of the first batch of men aged twenty to twenty-three, an estimated twenty-two in every 1,000 objected and went before local military tribunals. The tribunals varied greatly in their attitudes towards conscientious objection to military service and the proportions totally rejected ranged from 6 per cent to 41 per cent.

Desertion from the Armed Forces was a common problem. At one stage in the war there were over 24,500 men who were wanted for desertion. The problem of desertion became worse when soldiers knew they were about to be sent abroad.

Official figures show that large numbers of men due to take part in the D-Day invasion deserted. 36,366 of these soldiers were arrested between 6 June 1944 and 31 March 1945 by the Military Police; of these, 10,363 were charged with desertion.

Bert turned eighteen on 27 March 1943 and was called up for military service later that year. He had no thoughts of avoiding conscription, even though he would have preferred not to join the Army, but 'just accepted it' as something that he had to do. The summons came a few weeks after the medical examination, delivered by the postman in a plain brown envelope, with the instruction that the prospective recruit had to report to barracks for the start of basic training. Following an Army medical examination on 6 February at Prewett Street, Bedminster, he enlisted as Private 14600517 Herbert Henry Haddrell into the General Service Corps embodied Territorial Army on 6 May 1943. At the time of enlistment Bert's physical details are recorded as; height – 5ft 8½ins, weight – 122lbs, maximum chest – 34½ins, with grey eyes and light brown hair, having been medically classified as A1 Category. Posted to the 64th Primary Training Wing, he was required to report to Goojerat Barracks at Colchester, Essex – a primary training centre – where he completed his sixteen weeks initial training. Colchester was a large garrison town and the home barracks of the 4th Infantry Division. Resident units at the outbreak of war on 3 September 1939 included the 2nd Battalion Lancashire Fusiliers, the 1st Battalion East Surrey Regiment, the 1st Battalion Oxfordshire and Buckinghamshire Light Infantry, the 5th Royal Inniskilling Dragoon Guards, the 17th/21st Lancers, the 27th Field Regiment Royal Artillery, the 30th Field Regiment Royal Artillery, and the 14th Anti-Tank Regiment Royal Artillery. The division deployed to France in 1940 as part of the British Expeditionary Force.

Issued with a rail warrant, Bert made his way, by himself, to Colchester by train from Temple Meads station in Bristol. A daunting experience for an eighteen-year-old who still considered himself to be a boy, rather than a man, who had never been away from home before. It was all very strange and Bert felt very lonely and homesick. Once called into the forces in wartime, individuals had no rights whatsoever. They were in for the 'duration of the present emergency' and the possibility of being able to go back home seemed very remote, if ever. New recruits, often little more than boys, were constantly told that 'you are in the Army now and you have no rights'. If recruits were given any leave it was considered a privilege and unless they passed their training course, they would have to retrain all over again until they passed. The psychological effect on this particular naïve youth of eighteen, and no doubt countless more like him, was devastating and depressing.

After reporting to the barracks, and feeling very low in spirits, Bert was provided with a meal prepared by the ATS (Auxiliary Territorial Service), as the Women's Service was then known. The ATS were designated the Women's Royal Army Service Corps (WRAC) from 1949 until 1992 when women were integrated into the regiments and corps and badged accordingly. Bert described the meal provided by the ATS as 'mess in a tin', but he ate it nonetheless as he had been travelling for a long time and was very hungry. The bare barrack room that was to become Bert's home for the next four months accommodated about twenty recruits, and was furnished with not much more than bunk beds and a stove. Once they had been shaved

Goojerat Barracks, Colchester, June 1947. Bert's introduction to the British Army took place on his arrival here in May 1943.

and kitted out – all within a few hours of arrival – the rookie soldiers all looked identical, even if, back in the barrack room, every man was still an individual.

On enlistment, new recruits were issued with their basic equipment and clothing, which Bert claims 'you were lucky if it fitted you'.

The clothing worn by the British infantry soldier of the Second World War was known as 'the utility battle-dress', and it comprised of a serge wool, waist-length jacket (blouse) and trousers. At the start of the war its appearance was based on a pattern introduced in 1937, but by D-Day most men wore the '1940 pattern', often called the economy issue, or austerity pattern that was introduced in 1942. A flannel shirt was worn under the jacket. Although they had no collar, there was a 'granddad' style neckband made of pale tan cotton. It was buttoned from the neck down to stomach with gunmetal or plastic buttons. The trousers were of a type introduced in 1941 and unlike earlier designs had no belt loops or straps at the bottom of the legs. But like earlier styles, there was a large patch pocket with an exposed plastic button fastening on one thigh and a small patch pocket with centre flat pleat slightly higher on the other side for the first field dressing. The '37 pattern could be worn in a number of different combinations to suit the needs of all personnel. These were known as Orders of Wear, which for the infantry was as follows:

**Battle Order** – Belt, bayonet frog, basic pouches (2), braces (pair), haversack, shoulder straps (pair), entrenching tool carrier (head and helve), water bottle and carrier.

The first item to be put on to the belt was the webbing bayonet frog for the No. 4 Mark II bayonet. On to the centre of the webbing braces was fitted the small pack (or haversack). Normally kept under the flap of the small pack was the rubberised cloth groundsheet. This had holes along the edges so it could be used either as a cape or a rudimentary shelter. Hanging below the belt on the right hip was the webbing frame for the water bottle. The entrenching tool carrier was clipped onto the back of the belt although the tool itself was soon found to be insufficient for the job in hand, so was frequently left out; the carrier being used to hold personal items. The water bottle itself was made from enamelled metal with a khaki felt cover; it held two pints of water and was sealed with a cork on a short length of corded string. Frequently the soldier's enamelled tin mug was threaded through one of the straps on the small pack. Another piece of equipment suspended from the belt was a jack-knife. This was attached by corded string with a loop at each end and usually kept in a pocket. The knife, introduced in 1932, had a hard black plastic grip, a large blade, a short screwdriver and a tin/bottle opener. Either slung over the shoulder on its strap or clipped onto the belt by means of two hooks at the back, was the respirator case made from drab green waterproof canvas. Inside was the Light Service Respirator (introduced in 1941) as well as a cardboard envelope with six acetate eye shields; anti-fogging compound and rag; a tin containing five tubes of decontamination ointment, and two khaki gas detection armbands that turned red in the presence of gas.

**Marching Order** – This was normally reserved for either training or if the battalion vehicles could not follow. It was the same as above except the soldier would wear his 1908 pattern large pack on his back and his small pack hanging from its strap on the left shoulder in place of the entrenching tool. Inside the large pack, the soldier could carry cold weather kit, spare boots, etc., whilst a blanket rolled inside the groundsheet could be tied over the top. For cold weather, the soldier had his heavy 1940 pattern greatcoat. This was a knee-length double-breasted coat with a beige cotton or flannel lining sewn to the shoulders and reaching down to the chest. The only insignia allowed to be worn on these were the rank insignia and arm of service strip. However, a wool-lined, sleeveless leather jerkin was preferred for combat, as it allowed greater freedom of movement. He could also carry a balaclava helmet, woollen cap comforter, gloves and scarf.

For cooking, a soldier carried a set of two aluminium mess tins with thin folding handles that were poor conductors of heat (so the soldier did not get burnt), one fitting inside the other. These could be used for cooking, holding food or liquid. When not in use they could also store spare rations. To actually cook food, there was a small metal folding stand onto which a solidified alcohol tablet could be placed and lit. Over this, the mess tin was placed. He would also carry a set of cutlery and a pocket tin opener.

Braces – These were 'Y' shaped and made from white or khaki elasticated cotton. Each end terminated in a double leather tab for connecting to buttons on the inside of the battledress trousers. Metal fittings on the two front straps allowed for length adjustment.

Haversack (small pack) – This was worn either on the back in Battle Order or on the left side in Marching Order. A T-shaped fabric divider sectioned the inside of the pack, so that there were two small sections at the front for the water bottle and mess tins and a larger section at the rear. The official contents for this were: a small towel, mug (usually carried outside on one of the straps – sometimes in a sock to limit noise), rations, change of underwear, candle, matches/lighter, cap (when not worn – either FS (Field Service) or GS (General Service) type, Dubbin and brush, two spare handkerchiefs, pencil, gas cape, mess tin, knife, fork and spoon, change of socks, foot powder, Elastoplast (often wound round the pencil), safety pins, nails, shell dressing, bandoleer of fifty rounds of .303 ammunition, wash roll, housewife, spare chocolate, spare cigarettes.

Wash Roll – A piece of white linen with a pocket at one end and several loops down the middle for securing its contents. Typical contents included: soap in a holder, bar of shaving soap, comb, metal mirror, horsehair shaving brush, safety razor (metal or Bakelite), eating utensils, spare boot laces, a large oval brush for hair, a smaller one for clothing and a rectangular one for his boots. There was a toothbrush with nylon bristles, toothpaste and soap in an aluminium soap tin as well as white cotton face flannel. To clean his boots the soldier carried a tin of Dubbin and a tin or cake of Blanco to clean the webbing (this was sometimes carried in the entrenching tool holder, along with the brush). There was a guard for cleaning buttons made from pressed fibre or brass as well.

First Field Dressing – All troops were issued with a First Field Dressing that was normally carried in the specially-designed pocket at the front of the battledress trousers and also under the helmet netting. Issued in pairs and cellophane wrapped, each one was a 2x3.5in gauze pad that was stitched to a bandage.

Shell Dressing – The Shell Dressing was a 5.5x3.5in gauze pad and was for use on larger wounds or for binding splints.

Housewife – Although others carried out major clothing repairs, the soldier was expected to make all his own minor repairs. For this reason, each man was issued with a housewife, the standard issue sewing kit. Normally it was a white linen bag that contained the following: six brass and six plastic buttons, five sewing needles on a card, grey balled darning wool for socks, a card with 50yds of khaki thread and a plastic thimble. Because the battledress material was so tough, a small denomination coin such as a farthing could be found in the bag, to help push the needle through. As well as issue ones, private purchase housewives, of khaki or green material, could be often found. It was often colloquially called a 'hussif'.

Army Book 64 – The AB 64 was a small booklet that every soldier carried at all times and was his pay book and record of military service. Normally passes, ration coupons, etc., were carried inside for protection. The first section carried all the personal information such as Army number, surname, Christian name, date and place of birth, nationality of parents, enlistment date and the establishment joined. Further sections recorded the owner's training history, a record of trades and classes, specialist training, medical history (including sight tests, dentures, vaccinations, etc.) and last will and testament.

Equipment and clothing statement – Known as the 'kit book', this was a record of all the uniforms, weapons and equipment issued to a soldier. Everything received was itemised and initialled by the soldier and the quartermaster.

The recruit's day started at 0700 hrs with breakfast at 0800, followed by the first parade of the day. Drill was carried out within the barracks on a daily basis and, not surprisingly, Bert was not very good at this in the beginning. However, by the end of his basic training his drill had improved considerably, no doubt as a result of the extensive practice. The arena for the breaking-in of these young men was the parade ground. In squads they learnt how to obey orders instinctively and to react to a single word of command, whilst coping with a torrent of abuse from the Drill Sergeants. For the parade ground, boots were highly polished, having had the pebble-grained leather pressed to a smooth finish with a heated spoon before boot polish was melted and buffed into the boots. In the field polishing was not allowed. Instead, boots were coated with Dubbin to waterproof them. Every Saturday there was the Adjutant's Parade; the Colonel's personal staff officer, usually a senior captain, in charge of all the organization, administration and discipline for the battalion.

Varying in distance and getting progressively longer, route marches also occupied a significant amount of time for the new soldiers. At the end of marches, the band was always brought out to march the troops back in to camp. Marching, especially for those unaccustomed to it, made feet very sore and Bert used two measures to try and alleviate the pain. One method was to urinate in his boots prior to commencing the march in an effort to protect the feet, whilst the second method was to rub the feet with methylated spirits in an attempt to harden them.

PT (Physical Training) was carried out to improve the fitness of individuals. An important aspect of this was the regular sessions on the assault course. This included climbing over brick walls and poles, as well as having to go through water. On one occasion having run up a bank, Bert fell off and injured his ankle, resulting in being 'excused boots' by the Medical Officer for two weeks; which meant that he didn't have to put his Army boots on for a fortnight.

Weapons training involved being taught how to use the following arms and weapons, the rifle being the first weapon the new recruits received instruction in, followed by the Bren gun, then by the grenade, PIAT, anti-tank weapon, and mortar:

Rifle – The standard weapon of British troops was the Lee-Enfield bolt action rifle. The model used from late 1942 on was the No. 4 Mk. 1, similar in many respects to its predecessors first issued in 1888. Its box-type magazine, extending through the bottom of the stock forward of the trigger guard, carried two five-round clips of .303 ammunition. The Lee-Enfield was the fastest operating bolt-action rifle in the world. The rifle was sturdy, accurate and could be fired rapidly. A trained soldier could fire ten rounds per minute and be effective up to 900yds, although ranges up to 600yds were more common. Various sights could be fitted and it could also launch a grenade from a cup adapter or discharger. A superior locking system and easy field maintenance made the Lee-Enfield better than most other bolt-action rifles. Bert had never handled a firearm prior to joining the Army and the first time he fired his rifle, the strong recoil knocked him backwards.

Bren gun – The Bren gun, ubiquitous in British and Commonwealth armies, formed the basis of firepower of the infantry company, being used in rifle sections and also as a vehicle-mounted weapon on universal carriers (often referred to as Bren gun carriers). A gas-operated weapon, the Bren used the same .303 ammunition as the standard British rifle, the Lee-Enfield, firing at a rate of between 480 and 540 rounds per minute (rpm), depending on model. The gun was fired either shoulder-controlled from a bipod, or from a 30lb (13.6kgs) tripod, with which it could be used either in a defensive role, where the machine gun was mounted relatively low, or in a different manner as an anti-aircraft weapon. It was possible to choose between single rounds and an automatic mode. The Bren had an effective range of around 600yds (550 metres) when fired from a prone position with a bipod. In general, the Bren was considered a reliable and effective light machine gun. Its thirty-round magazine was, in practice, usually filled with twenty-eight or twenty-nine rounds to prevent jams and avoid wearing out the magazine spring. The Bren was officially operated by a two man crew – a gunner to fire and carry the Bren, and a re-loader to reload the gun and replace the barrel when it overheated. The re-loader carried extra ammunition and barrels. During wartime, however, the two man crew concept was abandoned and the weapon was commonly operated by one man, the gunner.

36M Grenade – The 'Mills Bomb' was a classic design; a grooved cast-iron 'pineapple' with a central striker held by a close hand lever and secured with a pin. Although the segmented body helped to create fragments when the grenade exploded, according to William Mills' (the designer) notes, the casing was grooved to make it easier to grip and not as an aid to fragmentation. The 'Mills' was a defensive grenade; after throwing the user had to take cover immediately. A competent thrower could manage thirty metres with reasonable accuracy, but the grenade could throw lethal fragments further than this. It could be fitted with a flat base and fired with a blank cartridge from a rifle with a 'cup' attachment, giving it a range of around 150 metres. At first the grenade was fitted with a seven-second fuse to accommodate both hand and rifle launch, but during combat in the Battle of France in 1940 this delay proved too long – giving defenders time to escape the explosion, or even to throw the grenade back – and it was reduced to four seconds.

PIAT (Projector, Infantry, Anti-tank) – The PIAT was a simple, short-range infantry anti-tank weapon made possible by the development of hollow or shaped charged projectiles. The PIAT round was propelled by a huge spring and spigot which ignited a cartridge within the tail of the projectile. Heavy and awkward to handle, it was difficult to load and kicked violently when fired. It was, nonetheless, very effective given the right circumstances.

Mortar – The 3-inch mortar was the standard heavy mortar used by the infantry battalions' support company to provide extra firepower. It could lob shells into enemy positions from a high angle and could hit targets from as close as 125yds to a maximum of 2,800yds. A crew of three transported it in a universal carrier and handled it as three separate parts: the smooth bore barrel, the base plate and the mounting which supported the barrel providing elevating and transversing adjustments. Once set up, a 10lb bomb was dropped down the barrel and hit a striker stud which fired a propellant cartridge in the tail of the bomb. When the bomb landed, a striker in the bomb set off its explosive. Three types of mortar bombs were used: smoke, high explosive and star.

Whilst the bayonet charge may have become a symbol of the First World War, its use did not die in the trenches of northern France, as bayonet training was still a major part of infantry drill during the Second World War. However, the weapon's use was encouraged more for psychological than practical reasons to keep men moving forward. In the words of C.J. Twine, in a wartime booklet published in 1942, bayonet training 'develops a high standard of co-ordination between mind and muscular action, a fine sense of control, a quick eye and an ever-aggressive spirit.' Bert's bayonet drill, he recalls, consisted for the most part of the new recruits charging and stabbing at suspended stuffed sacks.

Warrant Officers and Non-Commissioned Officers (NCOs – Sergeants, Corporals and Lance-Corporals) carried out basic training and were very strict, particularly the Regimental Sergeant-Majors (RSMs) and Company Sergeant-Majors (CSMs). Training always included lots of shouting from the instructors, with much 'spit and polish' in preparation for regular kit inspections carried out by the Company Commander. 'Blanco' was applied to gaiters and belts, all brass cleaned and spare boots polished. To carry all this equipment, a lightweight harness system made from web, a strong-woven cotton material, was worn. Webbing came in sand colour as standard and to change it meant coating it in the immortal Blanco. This was supplied in blocks or as a powder and came in No. 3 khaki green (for North-West Europe) or white (parade). To apply Blanco was a messy business. From powder, the webbing first had to be moistened, and then the powder could be applied with a wet brush. 'Blancoing' webbing from a block was much more difficult, as before it could be put on the web, it was necessary to turn the block into a paste. This could be done either by rubbing a wet brush on the block or by melting it in a little water before applying it to the web. To keep the webbing clean it was first brushed with a soft brush to remove any mud, and then carefully washed in soapy water (without scrubbing) before rinsing well and drying. Brass fittings on the webbing and buttons were highly polished (inside and out) in the depot or for the parade ground. This was done with brass paste and a soft brush; a Bakelite or brass button stick was used to protect the uniform or webbing. However, in the field fittings were allowed to dull so as not to reflect the sun. Uniform brushes were issued for cleaning the battledress, having first allowed the mud or other stains to dry first.

Rifles, which were carried at all times when training, had to be spotlessly cleaned, as the first event of the day was a close inspection of equipment, which was laid out in a specific order on the bed. One trick Bert and others employed was to buy a spare cork for the water bottle, as they had a tendency to rust, and only use the spare cork for kit inspection. Anyone not having his kit up to standard was put on a charge and had to report to an officer. The punishment could be seven or more days confined to barracks and having to report to the guardroom where the soldier was allocated two hours of chores, such as washing floors or sweeping up debris.

In addition to physical and weapons training, recruits received weekly current affairs education from the Army Bureau of Current Affairs. The ABCA was an organisation set up to educate and raise morale amongst British servicemen in the Second World War. ABCA issued pamphlets in units and promoted discussions, about, for instance, post-war reconstruction and the Beveridge Report, which dealt with health care and pensions schemes for post-war Britain. The publications, published fortnightly and containing a dozen or so pages of information (propaganda) on the progress of the war, were designed to give the fighting man an insight into the reasons why he had been sent to war. It met with resistance from Winston Churchill, who felt it was a poor use of military time.

Evenings were normally spent in the NAAFI canteen (the Navy, Army and Air Force Institute was formed on 1 January 1921 to look after the welfare of Britain's fighting men). Here soldiers could spend their pay on subsidised goods, chatting over a glass of beer or a cup of tea and a bun, Bert preferring tea as his favourite tipple. There was no entertainment provided in the NAAFI canteen, furnished with just a few easy chairs and perhaps a dart board, but Bert never ventured out into Colchester to pass his recreational hours.

On completion of his basic training, Bert joined the Dorsetshire Regiment on 17 June 1943 and was posted to the 14th Infantry Training Centre. He joined the regiment at Margate where the whole draft were billeted in private houses, sleeping about four to a room on paliasses (straw-filled bags), euphemistically referred to as 'donkeys breakfast'.

On 8 September 1943, Bert was posted to the 4th Battalion, the Dorsetshire Regiment, joining his unit at Bexhill-on-Sea, where the battalion had been stationed since 4 August following a four-month stay at Cliftonville. A publication by the Bexhill Museum Association about Bexhill during the Second World War provides an interesting description of the town during that period.

The Second World War caused the evacuation of Bexhill's schools and substantial bomb damage to the town, wrought during thirty-one raids by the Luftwaffe. As 1944 dawned, the invasion of Europe was anticipated with excitement and some trepidation in the town. Although some of the civilian population had returned to the town following the 1940 evacuation, nearly all the larger buildings, schools and some private houses were still requisitioned by the Army. The number of troops stationed in the Bexhill area continued to increase and by the late spring numbered a few thousand. The 4th Dorsets, the 7th Hampshires, their supporting Royal Artillery and service units were amongst the front line infantry units who were occupying the many empty school buildings and other large properties in the Hastings Road, Collington, Cooden, Little Common and Whydown areas and also empty houses in Glenleigh Park.

The cinemas, pubs, cafés and canteens were all crowded and the weekly dances at the De La Warr Pavilion were always sold out. Other dances and entertainment

Created in 1881 from the 39th and 54th Foot, the composition of the Dorsetshire Regiment's badge represents; the Castle and Key – the arms granted to Gibraltar by King Ferdinand II of Spain in 1502 – were a reminder of the 39th Foot's part in the defence of the Rock, while the motto *Primus In Indus* (First In India) commemorated the fact that the 39th was the first British regiment to serve in India. The Sphinx and 'Marabout' derived from the 54th's service in Egypt in 1801.

Private 14600517 Herbert Henry Haddrell, shortly after being posted to 'A' Company, 4th Battalion, the Dorsetshire Regiment. Below the regimental shoulder title is the Wessex Wyvern formation badge, and two horizontal red strips. Infantry battalions wore one, two or three red strips, one below the other to indicate the brigade to which they belonged.

events were also in great demand and usually packed with off-duty soldiers. Bert enjoyed his stay at Bexhill, going out into the town frequently for walks, visits to the cinema and 'in for a cup of tea'.

The troops were continuously engaged in advanced training and field exercises and the whole district had become a vast military camp and assembly area. All types of vehicles, from Jeeps and 15cwt Bedford lorries to Bren Gun Carriers and TCVs (Troop Carrying Vehicles) were scattered around the area, dispersed under any available cover in such places as the Highwoods and Gilham Wood and under the larger trees along many roadsides. These vehicles were draped with camouflage netting to render them almost inconspicuous to any enemy aircraft which might be passing overhead. The level of activity gradually intensified and all suitable garage accommodation, including part of the Drill Hall, was taken over for the task of waterproofing military vehicles. Work included the fitting of extensions to the exhaust pipes so the outlet was above the driving cab. This enabled the vehicles to be capable of driving through shallow water from the landing craft ramps onto the beaches. Throughout the war the sound of explosions and gunfire was almost a daily occurrence, with coastal defence guns, practice shots, mines being washed ashore on the beach and troops carrying out field training in the surrounding countryside.

Whilst based at Bexhill, Bert volunteered for signals training when members of the battalion were asked if anyone wanted to go on the course. This specialised course included instruction in the Signal Lamp, also called the Aldis Lamp, a visual signalling device for optical communications (typically using Morse Code); wireless procedure and operation (No. 18 radio set) and D5 telephone; Morse Code; laying cables (telephone wires); semaphore; and switchboard operation. Eventually, Bert passed the signalling course but, despite enjoying the specialism, didn't become a signaller:

We went out on a scheme while we were doing signals training and it was getting dark at night. We'd laid the cables – part of the job was to lay the cables for communication – and the scheme finished and we were told to reel them in. I was told to reel a particular lot in, so I go merrily along reeling it in. When I got it reeled in, I looked around and everybody had gone. There were no lights; nobody; no nothing and I was in the middle of a wood.

I thought that I wouldn't be able to find my way out at night and I'd got two reels of cable and my rifle. So I laid down in the wood and stayed there all night and then when it was light I made my way out; I could find my way out onto the road. Once there I started walking back to Bexhill and part way along a jeep came along driven by an American soldier. He asked me if I wanted a lift, and I said yes, please and he took me back to Bexhill.

I don't know whether anyone had missed me – no one ever said they had –, but I went to the Sergeant Major's office when I got back. I always remember this, he was drinking a cup of tea and he offered it to me, which I thought was very nice. But they seemed quite amused that I had bothered to bring the two reels of cable back, but in my mind I thought that they were quite expensive.

I was excused duty that day, but I don't know whether they would have sent anyone out for me or not!

Kenneth Hay remembers an extraordinary example of the wonderful hospitality and kindness displayed to troops billeted in the town, including himself and his elder brother, Bill, a pre-war Territorial who had fought with the Essex Regiment in the Norway campaign of 1940. Kenneth had also joined the Essex Regiment, but together with his brother had been transferred to the 4th Dorsets and they now found themselves in Bexhill – a town of which they had never heard. Some of the troops were billeted in requisitioned houses in Jameson Street and one day after doing something hot and sweaty, he was enjoying a cigarette whilst sitting on a front wall in his denims, when he was beckoned by two ladies standing in the gate of a chalet-bungalow opposite.

The two ladies, spinster sisters named Holbrook, asked if Ken would like a bath, which in his state was 'manna from heaven'. They asked if he had a friend who would also like to come, but would they please not wear their boots. Taking his brother Bill, they soon discovered that they had no need for their own wash things as they had set out flannels, towels, bath oils, soap etc. Within a matter of days the sisters had completely changed their home around so the conservatory was fitted out with card tables on which numerous games such as draughts, chess, Monopoly and cards were played. The front room was for reading from their extensive book-shelves and playing gramophone records, and an upstairs room also contained four or five card tables, on which were writing paper, envelopes, pens and postage stamps.

The invitation to use the bath as well as use all these facilities was extended, through the Hay brothers, to all the chaps in the nearby houses and it became more popular than any canteen, for everything was free. The Misses Holbrook sat around talking to those who wanted to talk, making tea, coffee or soft drinks every so often and then, in the evening, producing sandwiches and cakes as supper. Despite the fact that some of the troops took unfair advantage of this kindness, crammed their cigarette cases and stole the stamps, the sisters' kindness even extended to arranging for a fleet of cars to take the troops to the White Rock Theatre at Hastings; as many as thirty went to see a production of *While Parents Sleep*. When the Dorsets were posted uptown it was easier to frequent the New Inn and the Sussex public houses rather than travel down to Jameson Road.

It was during the battalion's stay at Bexhill that their introduction to the flame-thrower tank came at Galley Hill, the high ground above the coast on the eastern edge of the town. The British Churchill Crocodile flame-throwing tank was intro-duced as one of the specialised armoured vehicles developed by Major-General Percy Hobart (Hobart's Funnies) and was produced from October 1943, in time for the Normandy invasion. 800 were built. The Crocodile kept its 75mm gun in the turret, and the hull-mounted Besa machine gun was replaced by the flame-thrower nozzle. 400 gallons of fuel and nitrogen propellant, enough for eighty one-second bursts, were stored in a 6½ ton detachable armoured trailer towed by the Crocodile. The thrower had a range of up to 120yds (some sources quote 150yds). The pressure required had to be primed on the trailer by the crew as close to use as feasible, as it could not be maintained for very long.

Ken Hay graphically recalls his encounter:

We were lined up along the top of the slope and the tank, on our right, spewed forth a whole lot of flame and smoke right across our front and as soon as it did so we had to charge forward across the burning ground. It was exceedingly hot work and when we emerged on the other side, we found particles of the stuff were stuck to our boots and still burning. We had to grab tufts of grass and wipe it off before our boots were damaged. It was quite an impressive demonstration of the evil of the use of flame-throwers.

Soldiers of the 4th Dorsets were to encounter the flame-throwing Crocodiles again six months later in Normandy, but in very different circumstances, when the battalion went into action for the first time.

Divisional Battle Schools taught anybody who had not been in action before the basic skills of infantry work, the experience of being fired on, and the experience of advancing under a live artillery barrage. When the attack on Normandy came, anybody who had not already been under fire, had been so at a divisional battle school before they actually landed. Battle training involved live ammunition being fired over the recruit's heads from the 'enemy' in front of them. Bert recollects being 'very scared' by this, and it seems he was not alone. Brigadier Hubert Essame, of the 214th Infantry Brigade, provides an interesting account of this exercise during Divisional battle training:

> The exercises with live ammunition on the South Downs reached the climax of realism. The artillery, 8th Middlesex, the machine gun battalion equipped with Vickers, and in fact all arms of the Division (43rd) took part. They constituted the nearest approach to the actuality of war possible in the absence of a real enemy. The infantry learnt how close they could approach the bursting shells; they became inured to the bullets of 8th Middlesex passing over their heads and the fire of their own Bren guns flanking their advance. Smoke in vast clouds enshrouded the Downs. They acquired the art of dodging splinters of their own three-inch mortar bombs and came to regard the devastating explosion of the 4.2's nearby as an essential element in any battle.

Bert recalls one such exercise:

> During training one incident I remember well – while doing a mortar bomb practice on the South Downs, we had to align our sights on a distant electricity pylon. My first shot hit in the middle and it bent over in half!

The 43rd Division's exercise 'Vulcan' in December 1943, a four-day scheme, involved the whole division advancing against elements of the 61st Division and the 31st Tank Brigade. For most of the exercise, all three infantry brigades were in action or potentially so. But for the finale of 'Vulcan', only 214 Brigade was committed, carrying out an attack on the enemy's main position.

The areas of Kent and Sussex in which the 43rd Division carried out intensive manoeuvres were very similar in character to the terrain in which they were to be bloodied in battle; the tangle of scrubby woods and muddy lanes in some ways resembled the *bocage* country of Normandy. Whether this was by design or accident, the punishing warm-up for war in Kent and Sussex certainly provided a payoff in the early stages of the North-West Europe campaign.

Whilst with the Dorsets, Bert became part of his company's Bicycle Platoon, despite having never owned or ridden a bicycle in his life, the idea was that bicycles could convey troops quicker than marching. For whatever reason, perhaps his ineptitude at cycling, Bert was not one of the Dorsets who carried their bikes into Normandy.

Regular leave was granted to all soldiers prior to going overseas and Bert took advantage of this travelling to visit his family in Bristol and on occasions to stay with his older married sister, Ivy Sturch, who lived in a flat in Paddington, London. Following one such Sunday visit to his sister's home, Bert returned to Victoria Railway Station, having been previously told the time of his return train, to find the gates locked and the station closed. Being unable to return to barracks and having no alternative transport, he stayed overnight at his sister's, returning to his unit the following morning. Brought up on a charge for being AWOL (Absent Without Leave) the punishment 'Admonished' was handed out to him, by a somewhat charitable officer, who considered that he 'was not used to London', much to the chagrin of the attendant Sergeant-Major. Travel warrants were issued to soldiers on leave, as well as a part food ration book to take home to supplement the families existing rations, which didn't have any allowance for the on-leave serviceman. Bert was granted ten-day leaves on two occasions, commencing on 25 August 1943 and 24 January 1944, and was due another ten-day leave in June which was cancelled as the battalion learnt that it was on its way to France.

On 4 February 1944, the battalion marched to Hastings, where the whole of the 130th Infantry Brigade was inspected by General Sir Bernard Montgomery, Commander-in-Chief of the 21st Army Group; on 12 May it was visited by the Prime Minister, the Rt. Hon. Winston Spencer Churchill, the Dominion Prime Ministers, and Field Marshall Sir Alan Brooke, Chief of the Imperial General Staff, who watched a demonstration by its Pioneer Battalion.

The 4th Dorsets was part of 43rd (Wessex) Infantry Division. Sometimes known as 'The Fighting Wessex Wyverns' or, by its opponents as 'The Yellow Devils', the division's history begins in pre-First World War times when it was formed as a West Country Territorial Army Division comprising part-time soldiers from the Wessex region of England. Following distinguished service in the First World War, the division was reformed in 1920 once again as a West of England Territorial Unit. In 1935, the division adopted the Wyvern (a mythical creature which combined the ferocity of the dragon with the cunning of the serpent and the swift strike of the eagle) as its badge of recognition; appropriate as the monarchs of the ancient kingdoms of Wessex since Alfred the Great displayed the Wyvern on their battle standards. However, many of the division, affectionately, but irreverently, called their savage heraldic beast insignia 'the Pregnant Prawn'. The blue badge bearing a yellow wyvern was fitting for a formation comprising units that came primarily from the old Kingdom of Wessex, with battalions from the Devon, Dorset, Wiltshire, Somerset and Hampshire regiments, although many 'foreign' elements were to join it during the savage campaign in Normandy as reinforcements from Berkshire, Essex and other counties.

The mythical Wyvern, divisional badge of the 43rd (Wessex) Infantry Division.

A schematic (see page 49) shows how the 4th Battalion Dorsetshire Regiment and its rifle companies formed part of the 43rd (Wessex) Infantry Division. Each Brigade had three Infantry Battalions. In addition to that shown, the division also included Reconnaissance, Machine Gun Battalion (8th Middlesex), Royal Artillery (RA), Royal Engineers (RE), Signals, Royal Army Service Corps (RASC), Royal Army Medical Corps (RAMC), Royal Army Ordnance Corps (RAOC), Royal Electrical & Mechanical Engineers (REME), Provost, Field Security and Postal Unit. (The Divisional Order of Battle can be found in Appendix 1.) It is important that the intimacy of association of the grouping of the supporting arms with the infantry brigade is understood. When the 130th Infantry Brigade, for instance, is mentioned as having achieved a particularly remarkable success, its affiliated units – Brigade HQ, three battalions, 'B' Company One Heavy Mortar Platoon, the 112th Field Regiment, the 233rd Anti-Tank Battery, the 553rd Field Company, the 130th Field Ambulance, One SP Troop 362 LAA (Light Anti-Aircraft) Battery – equally share the honour.

The fighting elements at the sharp end of an infantry battalion were the rifle companies and the specialist platoons of Support Company, i.e. the 3in Mortar Platoon, the Carrier Platoon, the Pioneer Platoon and the Anti-Tank Platoon. These units, however, were totally dependent on logistical support if they were to function effectively. They needed re-supply in ammunition, reinforcements to replace casualties and perhaps above all, food. Such support within the battalion was organised by creating two echelons 'A' and 'B' which started from the rear echelon 'B' and worked forward. The Battalion Quartermaster commanded 'B' echelon. Here responsibility lay in accepting and checking supplies of all battalion necessities brought forward by lines of communication to the troops. Here too were kept the luxuries of life, for instance, clean best clothing and other indulgences, which could be brought forward

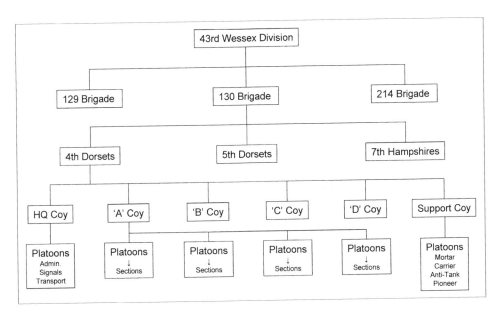

Basic organisation of the 43rd Wessex Division.

to 'sharp end' units where they were withdrawn for short periods of rest and retraining. In a situation of rapid advancement, 'B' echelon could often find itself twenty miles or more behind the parent battalion.

'A' echelon was much nearer to the 'sharp end' units. Its function was to accept the logistical necessities forwarded by 'B' echelon and to distribute them through to the fighting units, having broken down the requirements of each individual unit. Here could be found the cooks and colour sergeants of the companies who would prepare and distribute food to the forward companies and their supporting units when in action; also to ferry other essential supplies such as ammunition. Heavy battalion transport was located at 'B' echelon (the 3 ton vehicles); lighter transport (i.e. 15cwt), at 'A' echelon. When a battalion was in action, 'A' echelon was usually between two to six miles behind the front line.

The 43rd was a first-line Territorial Division in the UK at the outbreak of war. It was reorganized as a mixed division (i.e. with one armoured and two infantry brigades) in June 1942 and re-converted to an infantry division in September 1943. The division landed in Normandy on 24 June and took part in the bridgehead battles before fighting as part of the 21st Army Group throughout the remainder of the North-West Europe campaign. Immediately after the war, it formed part of XXX Corps District in the occupation of Germany. The division retained the same commander, Major-General G.I. (Ivor) Thomas, from March 1942 to the end of the war and was recognized as one of the most effective formations in the 21st Army Group. By the spring of 1944, 43rd Division had completed its concentration around Battle, Hastings and Rye. All leave stopped on 6 April. Field censorship of letters started. Banking accounts were closed and money drawn from field cashiers. Exercises continued. The Wessex Division waited in readiness to move.

# Chapter 4

# Normandy

On 2 June the Commanding Officer (CO) of the 4th Dorsets, Lieutenant-Colonel H.E. Cowie, addressed the whole battalion on points brought out by General Montgomery at a recent conference with unit commanders, regarding the move overseas. The previous day a carrier pigeon had been released by the battalion with a message to the Mayor and citizens of Dorchester, denoting the opening of 'Salute the Soldiers' week. 'Salute the Soldiers' week was a fundraising scheme to encourage civilians to save their money in government accounts, such as War Bonds, Savings Bonds, Defence Bonds and Savings Certificates. Cash could be paid into Post Offices or banks. In much the same way as 'War Weapons' week, it coincided with a week of parades, exhibitions and other war paraphernalia. In 1944 it was decided the national scheme would be themed around raising funds to equip an army that would be good enough to take on the German Army on their own ground.

The ban on troops travelling outside the battalion area and the six hours notice to move status was lifted for twenty-four hours on 3 June and the following morning, a Sunday, the battalion attended church parade at St Peter's, the parish church of Bexhill, the salute at the march past taken by the CO. Some degree of normality pervaded as preparations continued with an inter-company swimming competition taking place at Egerton Baths, won by 'C' Company.

On 6 June 1944, D-Day, the Allied armies made their first landings on the coast of Normandy, and the 4th Dorsets were ordered to be ready to move at twelve hours notice. On 7 June (D-Day plus one), the General Officer Commanding 43rd Division, Major-General Thomas held a conference, at the Ritz Cinema in Hastings, for all officers and warrant officers at which he explained the progress and intentions of the Allied Expeditionary Force (AEF). 43rd Division intelligence summaries were issued which contained details of the landing area in Normandy, together with topographical notes, with comments on the German Order of Battle, enemy defences, the French police and the attitude of French civilians. He closed his briefing by telling them that on the Continent they could dress as they pleased. He himself was to adopt singularly distinctive attire; high oiled boots, light-coloured riding breeches, battle dress blouse, cap with faded red band, and, in winter, a leather coat! As the new British Expeditionary Force was being assembled to make the first push into occupied France, a writer on secondment from the Intelligence Corps to the French section of the Political Warfare Executive was drafted to write a 'little pamphlet' which would be issued to troops preparing for the invasion. The pamphlet served as an introduction to France and the French people, and as an explanation of what the BEF soldiers should expect to find on the Continent – and as a result, it contains a good deal of advice and caveats about what kind of behaviour would and would not be appropriate. Containing candid descriptions of this war-ravaged society, as well as useful phrases and a pronunciation guide, it was an indispensable guide to every-day life. In 1944, the British War Office distributed the handbook to British soldiers informing them what to expect and how to behave in a newly-liberated France.

The codeword 'Mary', sent out from Divisional Headquarters at Tenterden in Kent at 6 p.m. on 12 June to all units, placed the 4th Dorsets at six hours notice to move, and on 14 June came the order to move to the battalion marshalling area. All ranks of the battalion were allowed out in the town of Bexhill-on-Sea until 2200 hrs that day. Even at this stage Bert, aged nineteen years and three months, didn't know where he was going. 'The rules were relaxed a little to give the troops a chance to relax. There was entertainment available and we were allowed to go out, but I didn't'.

Since the end of May, the whole division had been consigned to a number of battalion 'sealed camps'. A sealed camp meant that no one, but no one, was allowed out – in case someone unintentionally gave away the plans of the Allied commanders. The sealed camp complex was essential to security but it was psychologically uncomfortable for the internees. An additional irritation to all of those in 'internment' was the rigorous censoring of letters to families and other loved ones; in retrospect, a very necessary precaution.

The battalion left Bexhill-on-Sea on 15 June, the vehicles to embark at Tilbury on the River Thames, whilst the foot troops – the marching party – entrained at Bexhill Central Railway Station at 0904 hrs to travel westwards, although none knew where they were headed. Within a couple of hours, at 1400 hrs, they had arrived at the marshalling area, Camp C2, in the New Forest near Southampton, where they received a hot meal; an event noteworthy enough to be recorded in the Battalion War Diary. Whilst encamped under canvas in the concentration area, the battalion suffered two casualties before even arriving in France; one OR (Other Rank) became a casualty through falling in a slit trench during an alert, a second OR being injured during an afternoon football match.

At 1900 hrs on 17 June, the vehicle party embarked on SS *Ocean Angel* sailing in convoy from Tilbury at 2300 hrs, before anchoring off Sheerness. Two days later, the convoy was shelled whilst in the English Channel off the coast of Dover. Fortunately for the Dorsets, neither the ship nor any personnel were hit. The same day (19 June) that the vehicle party was being attacked in the Channel, the marching party left camp at 0830 hrs by lorry for the next stage of their journey to the Continent, embarking at Southampton on HMTS *Pampus* at midday with what they could carry on their backs. One company in each battalion embarked with bicycles. These caused considerable difficulties not only in getting up and down the ships' gangways, but also when the time came to disembark in landing craft.

Ken Hay, a recent transfer in April from the 2/4th Essexs to the 4th Dorsets, rec-ollects that the battalion — and possibly other units of the brigade — were on board HMTS *Pampus* sailing from Southampton that day. She was a 5,576 ton single-screw motor ship, newly-built in 1943 by Harland & Wolff's shipyard in Belfast as an Infantry Landing Ship. According to Ken, the *Pampus* was on her maiden voyage and as she sailed down the Solent there were lights from the shore signalling 'Happy Landings', 'Bon Voyage' and other signals indicating that it was her maiden voyage. Peter Hall, from Weston-super-Mare, sailing with the 1st Worcestershires considered the act of embarkation an awesome and exhilarating experience:

> There were more ships in the Solent than I had ever seen before — or expect to see again. There were Royal and US Navy cruisers. There was a multitude of troop trans-ports from the British and US Merchant Navies. All of the troop transports and most of the cruisers were suspending barrage balloons attached to hawsers from their main decks. Around this formidable armada, US and Royal Navy destroyers dashed around as if foraging foxhounds; sounding sirens which went 'Whoop! Whoop!' and flashing signals at the placid transporters embarking the men of the Division.

Bert Haddrell remembers:

> As D-Day approached we were sent to a transit camp at Southampton where we spent several days before setting sail for France. Bad weather kept us moored off France, but eventually we were able to disembark down over the side of the troopship and into small landing crafts — then to actually land in France. This was invasion and it was both frightening and dangerous.

Ever since D-Day the weather had caused anxiety. Fresh to strong winds, bad visibility and troubled seas had continuously affected the rate of unloading on the Normandy beachhead and limited air activity. In the early hours of 19 June (D-Day plus thirteen), an unexpected strong wind sprang up from the north making it almost impossible to work small craft in the assault area. Rapidly increasing as it veered to the north-east, the wind was blowing at over thirty knots by the afternoon, raising waves of 6-8ft. The storm continued to rage for three days, with winds increasing at times to gale force; no such June storm had been known in the English Channel for over forty years. The most sheltered spot was the British Mulberry Harbour off Arromanches-les-Bains. At Arromanches, where the Gooseberry breakwater was strengthened and extended by Phoenix caissons, the main breakwater, a line of sunken merchant ships together with concrete caissons, remained more or less intact and held back the worst of the gale. Damage to existing piers and pier-heads was considerable but not disastrous, and was mostly caused when out of control landing craft were driven against them.

In view of the storms then raging off the Normandy coast, the *Pampus*, with others, lay in convoy for four days in the gale in the Solent, off Spithead. Space was very cramped on the ship with so many men on board. In many cases the troops had to spend over forty-eight hours on the stuffy 'tween decks in an atmosphere which the smell of cooking soup did nothing to improve.

The Mulberry artificial harbour off the coast of Normandy, mid-June 1944.

When at last the storm abated, on 22 June, the whole invasion coast lay strewn with wreckage. Beached coasters and wrecked landing craft lay piled up at the high-water mark. Once the storm had subsided, Bert found the crossing was quite good, even enjoying sunbathing on top of the ship's deck. Disembarkation took place at night and required the battalion members having to clamber down nets on the side of the ship into waiting small craft, to take everyone ashore. Captain R.F. 'Henry' Hall, 4th Dorsets, describes his experience thus:

> There was a heavy swell off the beaches and to get into the landing craft from the mother ships we jumped into the boats off nets. As we scrambled down the nets on the side of the troop carrier, the landing craft was rising and falling about twenty feet. We had to let go and jump on when the LC was at the highest point! We moved off towards the beach and the silly Royal Naval chap who was running my assault boat got himself stuck on a sandbank about 150 yards or so off the waterline and he couldn't get himself off. So I thought, there's only one thing to do, and I said, 'Let down the ramp!' and I stuck my leg over the edge to try to feel the bottom to see how deep it was and I just couldn't touch the bottom. I said, 'Never mind chaps, it's my mother-in-law's birthday, off we go!' I jumped in, only to go down about two inches which really brought the house down. Laughing and joking we all jumped in and waded ashore. By that time the beachhead was quite secure.

Fortunately the rest of the battalion had a dry landing – just! Bert recalls nearly falling into 'the drink' as he clambered down the side of the troop carrier attempting to get safely into the waiting LCA (Landing Craft, Assault). Once on board, the LCA transported the infantrymen inshore. Some units of the 43rd Division were lucky enough to land under the protection of the Mulberry Harbour at Arromanches and had merely to walk down the long floating piers to the beach. The majority, however, came ashore in LCAs on the open beaches between Arromanches and Courselles-sur-Mer.

The 4th Dorsets marching party eventually landed at 0400 hrs on 23 June on the beach at Le Hamel, east of Arromanches-les-Bains, at the very spot where the 1st Dorsets had carried out the assault landing on D-Day. The section of Gold Beach where they landed was designated 'Item – Red'.

Unlike the D-Day assault divisions, the men of the Wessex following up landed in Normandy dry shod. The troops passed through the sand dunes and the line of huge concrete pill-boxes, past what remained of seaside villas, to assembly areas taped out in the trampled corn of the fields beyond. The Provost Company had done its work well. The familiar Wyvern signs and black arrows on a white background clearly marked the route to the division's concentration area. By the afternoon of 25 June, the whole battalion had concentrated in a field east of Planet, about a mile from the coast, and due north of Bayeux, where in fields and orchards they awaited the arrival of their transport and guns.

Bert recalled his first time on French soil, 'Once ashore the Battalion formed up and we started marching, before bedding down in the middle of a field.'

One company of each battalion in the second wave was issued with bicycles. Captain Hall's was one such company. 'We collected them at the head of the beach. Some Staff Officer must have thought that by this time the Germans would be run-

Landing Craft Attack (LCA) were used to convey troops from larger vessels to the Normandy shore or Mulberry artificial harbour.

The beach at Le Hamel, a few miles east of Arromanches-les-Bains, where the 4th Dorsets came ashore on 23 June 1944. Taken on 16 September 1945 by Private John Paradise who served with the battalion.

ning so fast we would need bicycles to keep up with them! We dragged them as far as Cheux – and then "lost" them in the mud!' At the concentration area north of Bayeux, the order to the 7th Hampshires was that all bicycles were to be dumped. The original order to 'dig a bloody great hole and bury those sodding bikes' was rescinded, and they were ordered to just make a big heap. Bicycles were coming in from other companies in the brigade until a heap was formed. If Bert had been more proficient at cycling during training with the Bicycle Platoon in England, no doubt this field in Normandy would have been the last resting place of his bike.

On 26 June, Montgomery launched the first major British offensive – code-named 'Epsom' – which lasted for five days. Montgomery's original timetable called for the Epsom offensive to commence on the morning of 23 June, but the delay in landing VIII Corps and the fact that the men were weary and seasick when they finally landed left the Commander-in-Chief with no choice except to postpone the operation until the morning of 26 June.

When Montgomery wrote to General Simpson (Military Secretary) in the War Office on 20 June he made no secret of his concern:

My Dear Simbo:

This weather is still the very devil. A gale all day yesterday; the same today. Nothing can be unloaded. Lying in ships off the beaches is everything I need to resume the offensive with a bang. In particular I must have 43rd Division complete and more artillery ammunition. If I can unload these by tomorrow night then I am OK. If I cannot do so I shall have to postpone the attack which would be a great nuisance as every day's delay helps the enemy. I am now five days behind my estimated build-up, all due to bad weather… The real point is that the delay imposed on us by the weather is just what the enemy needs, i.e. time to get more divisions over here and we know some more are on the move. It is all a very great nuisance.

The basic plan for Epsom employed about 60,000 British troops of VIII Corps, fresh from England and only just landed, consisting of three divisions as yet untried in battle; the 15th Scottish, the 11th Armoured and the 43rd Wessex. The plan was to pierce a short, two-mile stretch of the German front and drive a deep salient into the rear of Caen. Only the 15th (Scottish) Division and supporting tanks were to be involved in the initial assault. The task of the 43rd Wessex, in reserve, was to follow up and take over, holding the ground won and widening the salient. Most of these men had never been in action before; they were the new Army that had been training in Britain for three years. The 'Great Storm' had delayed their arrival in Normandy and many had endured a ghastly Channel crossing. They had embarked just before the 'Great Storm' and had had to remain at sea until it blew itself out.

Normandy is dairy and apple-producing country and the country over which the advance was to take place resembled in many ways the richer parts of Devon. Fields of standing corn alternated with pastures surrounded by high hedges and old dry ditches. In the fields south of the beaches, there were hundreds of dead cattle; a result of the enormous firepower of the naval and aerial bombardment that supported the initial waves of the Allied invasion. The June sun had caused these pathetic carcasses to swell from internal gases and burst. Many of the minor roads and tracks were sunken, offering perfect cover to a resolute defender. Viewpoints were few in number and limited in range. The many small villages were strongly built, with narrow passages between the farms and houses and set amidst orchards.

The River Odon flows generally north-east toward its confluence with the River Orne in the southern suburbs of Caen. North of the river is rich, rolling farmland and numerous small hamlets, from which the ground slopes gently downhill to become heavily wooded around the Odon. To the south, the woods give way to far more open farmland which quickly rises to a deceptively high elevation shown on maps as Point 112,. On a clear day, Caen and the entire region can be viewed from here. Hill 112 (one-one-two) was a natural springboard for a deeper penetration south toward the high ground around Bretteville-sur-Laize, which dominates the western approaches to the Caen-Falaise plain.

During the morning and afternoon of 25 June, the 4th Dorsets CO (Commanding Officer) attended Division and Brigade conferences on Operation Epsom, followed by visits round the battalion companies, with the IO (Intelligence Officer), Lieutenant E. Andrews, to 'put all ranks in the general picture'. At 2100 hrs at a Battalion 'Orders' Group the CO gave out orders regarding the move to forward Concentration Areas and issued '4 Dorset Admin Order No.1 (EPSOM)', dealing with rations. 'Orders' Group or 'O' Group was a session at which orders setting out the tactics to be used in a forthcoming action were given to participating commanders. Most actions entailed multiple 'O' Groups, starting at the highest level and descending downward. A brigade planning an attack, for example, will have its first 'O' group called by the brigadier. He and Brigade HQ staff will brief Battalion commanders and the commanders of included supporting arms (artillery, heavy mortars, etc.). Battalion commanders then brief the company commanders, who in turn brief platoon leaders, who pass the information down to individual sections. What started as a broad-stoke tactical plan at brigade level had, by the time it hit the platoon and section stages, become a set of intensely specific tasks that had to be accomplished for the overall success of the plan.

On 26 June, in heavy rain, the battalion arrived at its concentration area between Saint-Gabriel and Vienne-en-Bessin, about six miles due east of Bayeux and about four behind the front line, and at 1330 hrs the following day relieved the Canadian Régiment de la Chaudière in the rear area of Putot-en-Bessin, about halfway between Bayeux and Caen. During the afternoon the Dorsets settled in amidst very muddy and showery conditions. Lieutenant McFee, 2 I/C Anti-Tank Platoon, discovered a booby trap attached to a German rifle whilst examining an enemy grave and set it off from a distance. This was the first booby trap encountered by the battalion. Earlier that morning, the battalion 'R' Group had been taken around the company areas by representatives of the Canadian regiment. Le Régiment de la Chaudière was assigned to the 3rd Canadian Infantry Division as a standard rifle battalion and was designated as a reserve battalion during the D-Day landings in June 1944. The unit came ashore at Bernières-sur-Mer, surprising the locals who hadn't expected to find francophone troops in the liberating forces. It was one of only two francophone units to participate in Operation Overlord, the citizens in Normandy being surprised to find that soldiers of the Chaudière spoke a dialect of French very close to that spoken in Normandy, but were puzzled by the regiment's name. The regiment participated in the Battle for Caen, suffering several casualties in the fight at Carpiquet airfield on 4 July 1944.

During the night of the 26th, the 43rd Division began taking over the ground already won so that the 15th Division could continue the attack, and at 5 a.m. on the 27th, the advance was resumed by the 44th and the 46th Brigades moving forward to take the northern slopes of the Odon valley. The 43rd Division had hardly taken over the St Manvieu-Cheux area when the enemy began making probing attacks. All of these were beaten off, though in the most serious attack, enemy tanks penetrated Cheux from the west.

At 1330 hrs on 28 June, the battalion was put at half an hour's notice to move to the area of the Odon bridgehead, but the move didn't happen that day and the battalion was stood down for ten hours at 2230 hrs. On the morning of the 29th the infantrymen of the 4th Dorsets were all beginning to settle down to soldiering, having learned what they thought the war was like, but in the afternoon the battalion moved to Cheux, about six miles west of Caen and three miles north of the River Odon. The country between Cheux and the Odon is very close, a lot of orchards, small fields, not the *bocage* but still very close to its topography. This area had been the scene of severe fighting, and the fields were strewn with dead and dying cattle and horses. The weather was very close and the smell was quite sickening.

As the 4th Dorsets were moving up to reinforce the 15th Division's 'Scottish Corridor' – a salient made in the German defences – the battalion's Signal Platoon Sergeant recalled that at 1500 hrs:

> We were travelling through the gun areas when we were ordered to halt and disperse, everyone wondered what was happening; suddenly we were shaken by a thundering roar, every gun in the area opened up. What a barrage, red flames and puffs of smoke from cleverly concealed guns could be seen clearly; rapid fire seemed to work like clockwork. We couldn't hear ourselves speak. Officers and NCOs shouted to the men, at the top of their voices; telling them to disperse and take up emergency positions, as we were informed that Jerry was putting in a strong counter-attack.

The battalion arrived in the area at 1840 hrs and almost immediately found out what war was really like, for the 5th DCLI was having difficulty in repelling an enemy counter-attack supported by tanks (the 19th SS-Panzer-Grenadiers belonging to the 9th SS-Panzer-Division 'Hohenstaufen'). The CO placed 'B' and 'C' Companies under DCLI command, holding 'A' and 'D' Companies in reserve in the orchards of Le Haut du Bosq, about half a mile to the south, as a counter-attack force to work with a squadron of Churchill tanks. Little reliable information was available about the whereabouts of the enemy, even though the area was mortared and shelled, the battalion suffering seven casualties. By 2000 hrs the situation had become very confused with parties of Royal Scots and Royal Scots Fusiliers beginning to arrive in the village and tank squadrons of the 11th Armoured Division forming up in the area of high ground.

At 2200 hrs the CO, Lieutenant-Colonel Cowie, went forward in his carrier to find out the true situation in front, and discovered that the survivors of the Royal Scots and Royal Scots Fusiliers, who had moved into the battalion area from the south, had formed an all-round defensive area astride the road about half a mile north of Granville-sur-Odon, and that they had the situation well in hand. On his return along the road towards Cheux, Colonel Cowie encountered 'A' and 'D' Companies whom he had ordered to move up before leaving the village. He now ordered them to return and double up with their corresponding DCLI Companies. During the night the battalion received a hot meal, and although the 4th Dorset area was fairly heavily shelled, the men were well dug in and suffered few casualties.

Bert remembers being under heavy artillery bombardment at night and how frightening the experience was, with men screaming as a result of the barrage. For protection, slit trenches were dug, which usually accommodated two soldiers, and were about 3ft deep by 4ft long and 18ins wide. Bert found it difficult to dig using an entrenching tool as he had never done any digging in civilian life and the Army had provided no training or practice.

After five days, both sides were equally spent and with the 11th Armoured Division badly positioned behind the Odon and casualties within VIII Corps already unacceptably high, a continuation of the offensive meant another costly battle for Hill 112. It was a price Montgomery was not willing to pay and, with the ultimate goals of the operation now obviously unattainable, he ordered Epsom to be terminated on 30 June.

At 0130 hrs on the 30th, the 5th DCLI moved out of Cheux and the 4th Dorsets took over the area, into which the 7th Hampshires and the 5th Dorsets began to arrive at 1100 hrs. A few German prisoners were taken, but the day was a quiet one apart from enemy shelling. At 1100 hrs on 1 July, the enemy again started to attack with artillery, but the attempt to break through was stopped by the forward troops, and the battalion was not engaged, though it captured four enemy snipers. There was heavy rain all night. On 2 July the battalion was ordered to be ready to move in four hours; it was relieved that night, moving out in heavy rain, and before midnight concentrated in the area La Gaule, about a mile to the north-east. It remained in this position for two days, suffered some casualties from enemy shelling on the 3rd, and the next day had its first bath since leaving England.

Sgt Walter 'Wally' Caines, Signal Platoon Sergeant at the 4th Dorsets Battalion Headquarters, kept a campaign diary:

> 2 July. The Battalion was relieved by 1 Worcesters. A few shells fell in the area, unit suffered several casualties, some badly wounded. The medical services were excellent. One could see wounded being brought in by stretcher-bearers, who would sweat in streams after their strenuous slogging to and from the RAP, a hundred yards away from Tactical HQ. One could hear the wounded moaning, sometimes crying with pain as they passed by. The boys would walk alongside saying 'Cheer up, mate' and stuff a lighted cigarette in their mouths. A 'cig' always helped soothe the pain; this was known to all. The Padre held a burial service and the battalion dead were put to rest.

> 4 July. Battalion organised a bath house in each Company area. I felt lousy and was literally stinking after having spent days and nights in filthy trenches without a proper wash.

On active service, sleeping was done on the ground or in slit trenches wherever and whenever possible. Field rations for sustenance contained Compo ration, hard chocolate, soup, and 'dog biscuits' to sustain the troops. Corned beef was a particular favourite of Bert, something that he has never tired of eating.

At midnight on the 3rd/4th, the Germans started to bombard the Odon valley with heavy concentrations of shells and mortar bombs. A number of shells falling in the battalion area resulted in three casualties; two killed and one injured. The battalion moved again on the night of the 5th, and by 0045 hrs on the 6th had relieved a battalion of the Herefords in a defensive position at Tourmauville in the extreme south of the salient across the River Odon; at that time this was the most advanced position in the sector, and the battalion had the enemy on two flanks. It suffered slight casualties from enemy mortaring. Offensive patrolling began immediately and was maintained throughout the 7th, on which day Corporal Snooks showed great bravery by going into an anti-personnel minefield to rescue three wounded men.

Sergeant Caines wrote in his diary:

> 5 July. Our line system not working for over two hours, because a junction box was faulty, shells had cut the line in several places. Several fighting patrols went out during

the night to put out of action several SP guns. One patrol suffered heavy casualties having bumped into a strong enemy outpost, several were killed on both sides, some badly wounded. Private Stroud, a newly classified signaller, was one of the casualties.

7 July. Sergeant Northover and three members of the Intelligence section were sent out to establish a FO (Forward Observation) post escorted by two snipers and to keep wireless contact. No report was received. At 1400 hrs Private Sibley, one of the snipers, returned running like hell, sweating like a bull. The whole of the section had been trapped by the Germans; all were wounded except for the two snipers, and were captured.

The Battalion War Diary records the incident, reporting that Sergeant Northover and Sergeant Morgan, two 'I' ORs (Intelligence Other Ranks) and two snipers went out at 0645 hrs. At 1100 hrs only Sergeant Morgan and one sniper returned, the Observation Post having been attacked leaving three ORs missing. In the late afternoon of the 7th a relief 'recce' party of the Royal Scots arrived, and during the morning the 4th Dorsets moved to the rest area of Le Mesnil-Patry, five or six miles behind the firing line, where it remained for two days resting, being provided with a hot breakfast in the early hours of the 8th.

# Chapter 5

# Operation Jupiter

The 43rd Wessex Division had been spared the tough battles of Operation Epsom. Now it was their turn. In pursuance of Montgomery's objectives, 43rd Division's mission was to break out of the Odon bridgehead, which now lay between Verson and Baron, and seize a bridgehead across the River Orne. In doing so, they would provide the Second British Army with a springboard to advance across the enticingly open country that lay beyond the river. In order to achieve this, the division would have to take the dominating and well-defended bulk of Hill 112 and drive south around the eastern side of the hill, through Château de Fontaine and Éterville, to the village of Maltot and the River Orne beyond. Major General Thomas' plan was for the 129th Brigade to clear Hill 112 and establish artillery observation posts on the crest-line, before falling back to defensive positions along the line of the Caen-Évrecy road, with the 130th Brigade on the left to clear the low ground. Both brigades were to be supported by Churchill tanks of the 31st Tank Brigade and Crocodiles from the 141st Regiment Royal Armoured Corps (RAC) of the 79th Armoured Division.

The operation was to be conducted in three phases:

Phase 1 – the 130th Brigade, with the 9th Royal Tank Regiment (RTR), were to clear a German salient in the area of les Duanes (la ferme des Daims), which was held by a company of SS-Panzer-Grenadiers. Capture of Château de Fontaine, which was the location of Battalion Headquarters, II./SS-Panzer-Grenadier-Regiment 22, would follow. To their right, the 129th Brigade was to take the high ground of Hill 112, a feature that commanded both the valleys of the Odon and the Orne.

Phase 2 – the 129th Brigade were to hold a defensive flank on Hill 112 facing south-west towards Évrecy on the northern slopes of the feature. The 130th Brigade, supported by the 9th RTR and Crocodiles, were to attack Éterville and Maltot. If possible, they were to follow up this success by advancing as far as the high ground to the south-east of Hill 112 in the direction of St Martin. Meanwhile, the 46th Brigade was to provide left flank protection by taking over Verson and relieving the 4th Dorsets in Éterville.

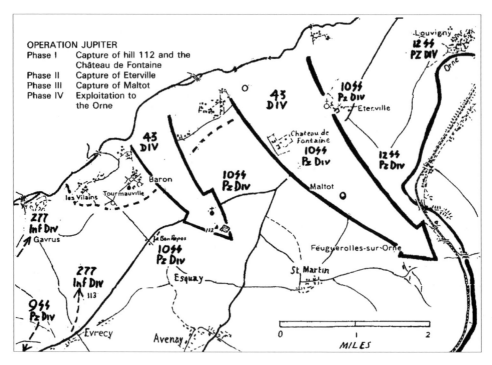

Operation Jupiter July 1944 – the 4th Dorsets first major engagement of the war.

Phase 3 – the 129th Brigade was to continue to hold its positions on Hill 112, while the 130th Brigade was to establish defences on the Éterville-Maltot line, facing the open flank to the east. At this stage, the 4th Armoured Brigade and the 214th Brigade were to be launched between the 129th and the 130th Brigades, south of the River Orne, and if the crossings were intact, form a bridgehead on the south-eastern bank.

The Top Secret code words for Operation Jupiter had West Country associations; Éterville and Maltot being 'Gloucester' and 'Bath' respectively, with 'Bristol' the code word for Esquay, the village on the western slope of Hill 112.

Apart from the capture of Hill 112, a ten-acre plateau that slopes away on three sides, the major role in the attack was thus assigned to the 130th Brigade. Circumstances up until now had, of necessity, kept this brigade in reserve. They had therefore been denied the advantages of gradual initiation into the realities of battle enjoyed by the other two brigades. The brigade plan was for the 5th Dorsets to seize the high ground around Château de Fontaine. When the château was secure, the 4th Dorsets were to pass through and capture Éterville. Finally, the 7th Hampshires with two companies of the 5th Dorsets would take Maltot and a small triangular orchard a little to the east of the village. Cheux had given the battalion its first taste of fire; it was now to fight its first major engagement and play its part in the great battle that was being fought for the possession of Caen. At 0115 hrs on 10 July it concentrated at Tourmauville, on the north bank of the Odon, in preparation for the attack on Éterville, and at 1535 hrs crossed the river and moved to an area immediately east of Miebord, suffering from enemy mortar fire on the way.

As the 4th Dorsets prepared to go into action, Bert was informed that he would be part of the cadre left behind as battle replacements, to follow on behind the action. A number of officers and men were always left out of battle (LOB), in case of disaster, to form the nucleus of the battalion. Taking Bert's place in the forthcoming attack was Private Bartlett. Bert's concern at the time was that because he was much taller than Bartlett, his greatcoat wouldn't fit him; the greatcoats had all been piled together. Bert was told not to worry about it. Private 5735215 Roy Bartlett was killed in action on 10 July 1944, aged twenty-one years, and is buried in St Manvieu War Cemetery, Cheux.

The brigade attack was opened by the 5th Dorsets, who captured the remains of Château de Fontaine and nearby farm, which had been the HQ of II./SS-Panzer-Grenadier-Regiment 22, half a mile to the west of Éterville. While 'C' Company of the 5th Dorsets was still securing Château de Fontaine, Brigadier N.D. Leslie, commanding 130th Brigade, launched the 4th Dorsets from the outskirts of Fontaine-Étoupefour against Éterville. The village was less than 700 metres from Horseshoe Wood, with a lane running north-south dividing it in two. To the west, the village's main feature was the eighteenth-century château and large farm complex. To the east of the road was another large farm and spread around the whole village were smaller dwellings, trees and cider orchards. The I./SS-Panzer-Grenadier-Regiment 22 held Éterville along with a company of SS engineers acting as infantry. The remains of the 1st SS-Panzer-Grenadiers were dug in on the ridge that extended from the village in a north-easterly direction towards Louvigny.

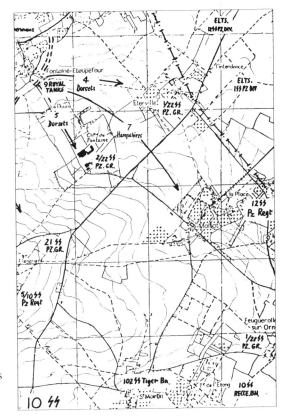

The attack by the 4th Dorsets on Éterville and Maltot was launched from the outskirts of Fontaine-Étoupefour against elements of the 1st, 10th and 12th SS-Panzer-Divisions.

At 0620 hrs the 4th Dorsets attack was opened by 'A' and 'B' Companies, on the right and left respectively, 'C' and 'D' being held in reserve. Advancing under an artillery barrage on a two-company front with a squadron of tanks and flame-throwing Churchills on the left flank, the troops went forward with a great dash and entered the long, straggling village. German infantry dug in on the first rise were quickly overrun. The Dorsets pushed on rapidly, leaving dead and wounded in the cornfields behind them. Enemy shellfire was falling, carriers and trucks burning. They reached the approaches to Éterville close behind the moving barrage. At first casualties were light. About seventy prisoners were taken and the battalion started to consolidate.

SS-Haupsturmführer Friedrich Richter, commander of the 1st Battalion 22nd SS-Panzer-Grenadiers, had spent that night visiting the forward companies in defence of Éterville. At dawn he and his company runner were on their way back to Battalion Headquarters when a torrent of British shellfire descended:

> It took us more than an hour to cover seven hundred yards. We arrived just as a messenger came in from our reserve position: 'Enemy tanks level with us across the boundary with 1st SS.' Off went SS-Sturmann Schwingel and the company runners with my orders: 'Pull back into Éterville immediately!' The artillery barrage was now deafening and smoke was being mixed with the high-explosive. Grenadiers arrived from Château de Fontaine carrying the seriously wounded commander of the 2nd Battalion. More and more wounded started to come in from 1st Battalion positions, and then Panzer-Grenadiers who had managed to get away when the Château de Fontaine defences were overrun.

Major G.L. Symonds, commanding 'B' Company has written the following account of the battle:

> Éterville is a small village situated in the high undulating land south of Caen, between the Rivers Odon and Orne. It is surrounded by trees and cornfields, and was easily identifiable from air photographs, although it was too deep in enemy territory for us to be able to see it before the attack began. The intervening country was principally under high standing corn, which made it difficult to pick out enemy positions, but afforded considerable cover for infantry. All this high ground, which lay to the south of Caen, was very strongly held by the Germans with several Panzer divisions, and was in fact Rommel's hinge position. The principal object of our attack was to contain as many enemy as possible in this sector, whilst the Americans were breaking out further west. The supporting fire programme was very heavy and included RAF and units of the Fleet firing from the Channel. 'B' Company, which I was commanding, was supported by a squadron of Churchill tanks – 'C' Squadron, 9th Royal Tank Regiment - and 'A' Company by a troop of flame-throwers – Crocodiles of 141/RAC, 79th Armoured Division. We began our approach march about midnight on 9 July, and arrived in the forward assembly area in the early morning, where we had a breakfast of bully beef and biscuits, and checked over our weapons, etc., although there was in fact little left to do, as we had been preparing for this very occasion for so long. Everyone was in high spirits, although of course a little apprehensive, as was only natural in such surroundings with dead and rotting men and animals, and destroyed farmsteads all round.

We formed up immediately behind the start line in a cornfield and were shelled a little whilst doing so, causing one or two minor casualties. At 0620 hrs Colonel Cowie gave the long awaited signal to go by having Lance-Corporal Butt sound the charge on his bugle. The battalion rose to its feet as one man, many cheered. It was a wonderful experience, and we were all glad at that moment to be there. As we breasted the top of the hill we overran a German platoon dug in the corn immediately in front of my company. They offered practically no resistance, surrendering immediately, and we continued the advance to the edge of the village, where we had to lie down and wait for the Artillery and the RAF to cease shelling and bombing Éterville. We were very close to the barrage, and still in excellent formation, having suffered only a few casualties from enemy shelling during the advance up to this time. The end of the supporting fire – which included fire from 5th Dorsets and 'B' squadron 9th Royal Tank Regiment in Horseshoe Wood – was marked by blue smoke shells, and I gave the signal to assault as soon as these fell. No sooner had we begun the assault than about four fighters [Typhoons] came over, presumably a little late, and dropped two bombs in the middle of my company whilst we were still in the open field. We could see the bombs falling so had time to lie down, but we suffered a number of casualties from these, including Sergeant Fowler, who was killed, and three of our number 18 radio sets were put out of action. The enemy began to shell and mortar us heavily.

Captain 'Harry' Hall also recalled the incident with the close support aircraft:

Typhoons were supposed to drop anti-personnel bombs on the village just before we entered but they were late! We took our objective at 0630 hrs as planned and planted our totem – a six foot holly pole with a brass jug which we had pinched from a pub in Sandwich and my whole patrol had scratched their names on it. On top of the pole was the skull of a cow! Before we had a chance to dig in the Typhoons arrived. My only casualty was Sergeant Fowler, my new Platoon Sergeant who was killed because he made the mistake of not staying standing up, watching the bombs coming down and dodging them, thus exposing only the legs to splinters – also a good defence against Nebelwerfers [German for 'smoke-launcher'] which you can hear coming if you are caught in the open – but he lay flat on the ground and therefore was killed.

Alfie Brown of 'A' Company, on the 4th Dorsets' right flank, was sheltering behind the bulk of the Crocodiles fuel trailer as they advanced within 100 metres of the edge of the village:

… when there was a rushing sound like a train and a loud 'wumf' as the hedge caught fire… black oily smoke was everywhere. I don't know if any Jerrys were caught but I saw some further along, running back from bunkers to the mansion. As a result we got into Éterville fairly easily, but that's when our troubles really began…

When Sturmann Schwingel burst into his unit headquarters at Éterville Château the shells were whining and whistling past overhead. Shells from British tanks were, however, soon crashing into the western wall of the German HQ building; the upper storeys were collapsing in showers of dust, stone and plaster. Solid shot broke through into the partly-raised cellar that housed the headquarters staff. The entrance hall was a confusion of wounded men being helped or being carried to the safer side of the building. Beneath the trees outside a large German signals truck was burning. Time was short. The Battalion Commander gave the orders to move out. But what of the wounded? The commander turned to the medical officer, SS-Untersturmführer Dr Horst Moeferdt, 'We can't leave them on their own! You'll have to stay!' To take care of the wounded Moeferdt had at his disposal two medical orderly staff; l'Oscha, Flüge, and a Rottenführer.

Told by his superior officer that would have to stay with the wounded as the English would not be able to look after them during the fighting, Dr Moeferdt had a hard time persuading his captors from 'A' Company, who had cleared the Éterville Château and found they had captured the I./SS-Panzer-Grenadiers 22 aid post with sixty wounded, that he and his medics should be allowed to stay and treat the German wounded:

> I couldn't understand what they were saying, but it was clear we were meant to put our hands up. All who could manage to walk were ordered out – not many other than the orderlies. My efforts to make them understand that I was a doctor, that I should be allowed to stay and look after the wounded, were to no avail.

It was the padre of the 4th Dorsets who intervened and released the German medical officer and the two orderlies. Oblivious of the falling shells, they worked on in coop-eration with the British medical staff. The wounded Germans were hoping that they would be released by counter-attackers from the divisional reserve counter-attack. However, no counter-attack reached the wounded SS soldiers who were evacuated as prisoners of war in Bren gun carriers. The wounded included SS-Sturmbannführer Hans Löffler, the officer commanding the II./Panzer-Grenadier-Regiment 22 who, bleeding heavily from shell and grenade wounds, had been attempting to leave in a medical vehicle for a field hospital, but the 'Sanka' (ambulance) was hit by a shell, forcing him to remain in Éterville where he was captured.

Once in the village the 4th Dorset's plan was for the leading companies ('A' and 'B') to fight through Éterville quickly and reach their objective, the main road at the southern edge of the village. Detailed clearance was the task of the reserve companies and these were to be followed at 0800 hours by the 9th Cameronians who were to relieve the 4th Dorsets and take over the defence of the village. Attacking on a two-company frontage, the battalion found that after breaking into the village 'A' and 'B' companies started to diverge left and right, as the two rifle companies were drawn towards enemy strong points. Advanced Battalion Headquarters, unu-sually, found itself in the front line, acting as a link between the companies. With the Advanced Battalion Headquarters was Sergeant Geoff Cleal, the battalion's chief clerk:

> As we arrived beside the church we were greeted by a barrage of shells. The thick walls surrounding the churchyard seemed to bounce outwards and then fall back into place.

The church became the Regimental Aid Post. Dug in tanks continued to pump shells into it killing wounded as they lay on their stretchers. Outside I recall two of us digging in Battalion Headquarters in front of the churchyard wall behind a tree, with the idea that each of us could lean on the tree to fire our rifles. The CO was about twenty yards away directing operations over the radio transmitter from his carrier. On the left, two other Bren gun carriers were on fire and ammunition in them was exploding every few seconds.

By 0745 hrs the 4th Dorsets were reporting that they had reached their objective and that Éterville was occupied despite being heavily mortared. In reality, however, the battle in and around the village was to go on all day and into the following night. The leading assault groups had indeed passed through the village without great opposition when the battle flared up behind them.

Major Symonds continued his account:

The weight of the supporting fire had been so great that the enemy offered no resistance at first, the assault coming before he had time to recover, and we reached our objective, the road beyond the village, without much difficulty. A number of Germans surrendered, some withdrew, and some had yet to be mopped up. The mopping up, which was done by 'C' and 'D' Companies, was not so easy, as the garden and field hedges were high and the foliage thick, and soon some enemy troops, who had been quiet to start with, opened fire on us. The enemy then began to shell and mortar us very heavily, and he kept this up all the time we were consolidating, making the whole job very difficult. The attack had gone quite a long way into the enemy positions and they were now very close to us on our immediate front. I could see 'A' Company, under Major Upton, on my right during the advance and assault, and with their Crocodile flame-throwing tanks in action they looked quite irresistible. They reached their objective on our right about the same time as we did, and probably in rather better order, as they did not get the benefit of our own bombs as we did. As 'A' Company was, later in the day, lost almost to a man at Maltot, I did not get the chance to ask any of them details of their battle at Éterville.

After consolidating the position and digging in, the battalion was subjected to heavy enemy mortaring and shelling, and suffered many casualties, including Major Gaye, commanding 'D' Company and Major Symonds who was wounded by a shell while digging his slit trench.

Sergeant Caines was also digging in:

Just before HQ reached Éterville, a hell of a barrage came down upon us, several were wounded. We were split up having to take cover. We then became somewhat disorganised. After some terrible minutes dodging shells and mortars, the odd few of us decided to remain until the barrage eased up and then move on. Shells were still raining down like hailstones. The battalion's casualties were pouring into the village church besides many Germans lying around wounded. Everyone was told to dig in for their dear lives' sakes. All we had with us was an entrenching tool, which proved useless; to speed up the digging several of us sifted the earth with our hands. The MO and his stretcher-bearers were working like niggers to dress the wounded. Our very brave Padre volunteered to

A section from one of 4th Dorsets Companies take cover from mortar fire as they await the call to move forward, Fontaine-Étoupefour, 10 July 1944. Frank Porter believes these are men of 8 Section, 3 Platoon, 'A' Company. (Imperial War Museum B 6852)

find a German MO to attend their wounded. An hour later to our astonishment he returned with an enemy MO and both worked alongside dressing the wounded. I have a vivid recollection of the efficiency of the German medical personnel whom we captured who worked hard at bringing in our wounded as well as their own…

The situation in the 4th Dorsets Regimental Aid Post (RAP) at the church was dire. The number of Dorsets casualties would have outnumbered the RAP staff and the attached RAMC field ambulance section on their own, but there were also an almost equal number of wounded SS soldiers needing treatment. Together, the SS and British medics worked to treat casualties of both sides, all the while under fire and in danger from falling masonry, as the shells gradually reduced the church to a ruin. Soon the RAP was overflowing with casualties, and soldiers of both sides were being wounded for a second time while they lay on their stretchers in the churchyard awaiting treatment or evacuation. Seldom have medics had to fight their battle to save comrades' lives in such harrowing circumstances. Soldiers and medics from both sides, who had worked together for many hours on that day, expressed mutual respect for their opposite numbers' professionalism and impartiality. For his personal example and leadership, the Battalion Medical Officer, Captain Thompson, was awarded the Military Cross for his courage in looking after the wounded under heavy shellfire. Captain Baker, OC Anti-Tank Platoon, with one leg completely smashed, somehow managed to drive a carrier back to the first aid post with other wounded aboard. The only approach for vehicles was by a sunken lane, which became blocked by the carriers, many soon in flames. The RAP overflowed with casualties, and could not be evacuated as no ambulance could reach the village.

As soon as it became apparent that the enemy had secured a foothold in Éterville, Grenadiers of the 12.SS-Panzer-Division, in reserve in the woods to the east of Maltot, immediately counter-attacked. This was standard German practice but, hastily developing into a fluid battle, their advance soon lost momentum amongst the hedges and buildings of Éterville. SS-Hauptsturmführer Richter and the German headquarters' staff were rallying groups of survivors in Éterville and from the Château de Fontaine. They were fighting back in the gardens and along the tall thick hedges of dense foliage. Machine-gun bullets were tearing across farmhouse walls in spurts of dust and splinters of stonework. Then down came the showers of German shells and mortar bombs that were always thrown at villages they had just lost.

SS-Hauptsturmführer Friedrich Richter:

Leaving the Château we took up positions at the rear edge of the village in a ditch by the edge of the road. Many had already retreated from the village to join the battalion reserve. We held this position for about two hours. We only had three light machineguns and rifles. We let the English infantry advance to within thirty metres. As they came through the long grass, we opened fire. They were all downed without exception. After this we were not under fire for a short time and we were free to disengage to the rear. Two enemy machine guns advanced from the Château but we had a head start and successfully retreated 1,000 metres towards the bend in the Orne. On the way back we were joined by stragglers from the 12.SS-Panzer-Division ('Hitler Jugend'), who had been holding the eastern edge of Éterville, and we soon numbered sixty-five.

At the far end of Éterville, Major Symonds had just sited his company in defence when he saw enemy Panzers and infantry across the fields in the direction of the river:

After I had got my company firmly on the ground and had got the carrier round with more ammunition for the platoons, I began to dig my own slit trench. I had only got the top soil removed when one of the hundreds of shells and bombs that were showering upon us tipped me into my own works. I was unconscious through loss of blood for a little while. However, when I came round I was still there, my Canadian second-in-command, Captain Ron With, had stopped the bleeding for me, and I was able to hand over to him the message that I had just received, to go to Battalion Headquarters for orders to attack Maltot almost at once, as the 7th Hampshires had failed to capture it. There are probably few people who know just why the 7th Hampshires failed to capture Maltot, but I witnessed one of the reasons. They were due to pass through Éterville to attack Maltot as soon as we were firm in Éterville, and this they did. As soon as they passed through us they ran into the German counter-attack, which was forming up about 300 yards beyond Éterville to try and dislodge us. I shall always believe that the 7th Hampshire's attack on Maltot, coming when it did, saved my company from being completely overrun before we were properly dug in.

For his part in the attack, Major Symonds was awarded the Military Cross. The citation read, 'By his personal example under shellfire, and in the face of the enemy he proved himself to be a real leader, and he continued to inspire and cheer his men even after he was badly wounded'.

The attack on Éterville had gone well; there is no doubt that the whole operation at Éterville was quite a model attack against a relatively strong enemy. The objective was reached on time but the German response of shelling and counter-attacks had slowed the progress of detailed clearance and consolidation. In addition, Headquarters of the 130th Brigade had underestimated the amount of time that even the well-trained 4th Dorsets would need in practice to clear a real enemy out of a built-up area. The main problem was that the strong-points that had been bypassed needed clearing by the following companies who had little idea of where it was safe to move and which areas were still covered by enemy fire. In the village, equally determined West Country and SS infantrymen fought a bitter struggle for every building. A platoon of Dorsets, about thirty men under Lieutenant Hayes, had disappeared in the confusion of battle; it would be several days before a night patrol would stumble over their dead bodies.

Brigadier Leslie's original plan was for the 9th Cameronians who had followed the 130th Brigade out of the Odon valley to relieve the 4th Dorsets some time after 0800 hrs, as soon as they had taken the village of Éterville. However, because of the intense shelling and fighting going on in the village, the handing over took place about midday. The regimental history describes the situation:

> Lieutenant Colonel Villiers halted the Cameronians in Fontaine-Étoupefour, about 1,000 yards from Éterville, while he went forward to contact the 4th Dorsets. The only approach for vehicles was by a sunken lane, which at the time was blocked by several of Dorset's carriers, all of which were in flames. The Dorsets were still fighting for possession of the far side of the village itself, which was continually being mortared by the enemy. As a defensive position Éterville was a tactical nightmare. Lieutenant Colonel Villiers decided nonetheless that the Cameronians must start taking over immediately in order to relieve the Dorsets for their next operation.

At 1345 hrs the 4th Dorsets were relieved by the 9th Cameronians, handing over twenty-six German prisoners to them, and reorganised in order to help the 7th Hampshires, who had suffered heavy casualties in the failed attempt to take Maltot. The Dorsets concentrated, as the 130th Brigade's reserve, near Horseshoe Wood. Bill Avery recalls that 'when we reached Rear HQ we were met by the QM Capt. Titterington with hot drinks. 'Wally' Caines also returned from Éterville:

> Several dead Germans lay around, one of which I shall always remember. As I was just sitting down, being practically exhausted... I saw beneath some long grass a dead Jerry. At first he looked alive, his face seemed to have plenty of colour and his body showed no distinctive markings of death. I was really afraid to touch him or go any nearer him, knowing too well what might happen, for we had all been drilled as to the possibility of dead bodies being booby traps. Grenades were stuck in his belt, his rifle in his hand and his helmet was still on his head, he had washed and shaved. I kept wondering: eventually I bucked up my courage and touched him to make sure that he was a dead one. Yes, he was all right, but whether he was booby trapped or not, I did not bother to find out.

# Chapter 6

# Attack on Maltot

At 1500 hrs, a commanders' conference assembled in the tower of Fontaine-Étoupefour Church. From here, Major-General Thomas and his brigadiers could see that the situation around Château de Fontaine and Éterville was far from quiet and Hill 112 had not been taken. Amongst the things decided at this conference was that the 4th Dorsets, who were now in reserve between Château de Fontaine and Éterville, should immediately move to the support of the 7th Hampshires in Maltot. Having been relieved at Éterville, the 4th Dorsets had barely two hours to reorganize after their heavy casualties and reload with ammunition before orders came to 'move now' to support the 7th Hampshires. There was little time to spend planning, companies were simply allocated quadrants of Maltot to reinforce, marry up with Churchills of 'C' Squadron 7th RTR and advance southwards. Little was known except that the Hampshires were still in the village, and there was to be no fire support from artillery.

Company Sergeant-Major Laurie Symes recalls the battalion's mood:

My company – 'D' – formed up for the attack on the reverse slope in front of Château de Fontaine waiting for the off. I was in the company Bren gun carrier which was loaded with the company's reserve ammo. Neither myself nor my driver gave a thought at the time what would have happened to that lot, if we had been hit by an 88 [88mm German anti-tank artillery gun]. The whole company had their tails up for this attack and were eager to go. I looked up the slope to see Major Eastwood, our company OC up front with his walking stick and whistle. When the time came, off we went through the standing corn.

By 1535 hrs the battalion had formed up at the FUP (Forming-up Point) and at 1620 hrs the attack on Maltot began, supported by tanks, against terrific opposition from a Panzer division. The Dorsets' move coincided with the final act of the 7th Hampshires' defence of Maltot. As the 4th Dorsets approached the village, they met the remnants of the Hampshires withdrawing from the ruins. In a recording made in a captured German trench, somewhere on the ridge between Éterville and Maltot, the BBC news reporter, Chester Wilmot, recorded these words while looking down the northern outskirts of the village:

By now that wood was enveloped in smoke – not the black smoke of hostile mortars but white smoke laid down by our own guns as a screen for our infantry who were now being forced to withdraw. We could see them moving back through the waist-high corn and, out of the smoke behind them, came angry flashes as the German tanks fired from Maltot. But even as the infantry were driven back another battalion was moving forward to relieve them, supported by Churchill tanks firing tracer over the heads of the advancing men. They moved right past our hedge out across the corn. The Germans evidently saw them coming, for away from our right flank machine guns opened up and then the Nebelwerfers…

'Wally' Caines recalled the advance in to the village:

Tigers were concealed in orchards, and machine-guns fired from all angles. Most of our attack vehicles were knocked out by 88s. Our anti-tank gunners did not have time to place their guns in position. The main body of tactical headquarters were moving towards the village crossing a cornfield on the outskirts. Jerry must have observed every move, and allowed us to come right up close, thus cutting us off. Suddenly the whole party was cut down by a burst of fire from a Spandau [German machine gun]. It was hell, no one dared raise his head above the corn, as soon as Jerry observed the slightest movement a burst of fire would be the reply. This firing kept up for some time, everything seemed to open up together, self-propelled guns firing practically unceasingly.

Sergeant Geoff Cleal, still with Advanced Battalion Headquarters, remembers vividly:

During the advance to Maltot we were pinned down in standing corn, some of which was burning. Every time we made the slightest movement, we were greeted with a burst of machine-gun fire. It was frightening to hear the bullets hitting the corn above my head.

Bill Avery, 4th Dorsets, had a similar experience:

We formed up again to go into Maltot to assist the 7th Hampshires. The CO went forward on foot, and then with Fred Harris we went forward through the cornfields with the Adjutant's radio truck. The corn being waist high and being covered by German machine gun crossfire, the lads were keeping their heads down.

The high-velocity 88mm cannon of the Panzers opened up to the right and left of them. A blinding flash in the corn, and men were lying killed and wounded before the sound of the gun had reached them. A dull thud, a fountain of earth thrown into the air, and a Churchill tank was in flames. Carriers and anti-tank guns were being torn apart. The few Churchills not sending spirals of smoke into the air ran for the safety of the ridge behind them.

Lance-Corporal Chris Portway recalls the horror of the 4th Dorsets' second encounter of the day with their own airforce's ordnance:

A squadron of rocket-firing Typhoons dropped out of the sun in twos and threes with the noise of an express train: the field seemed to rise up in flames; there was a great noise of rending metal. Rooted to the spot, we gazed upwards as another plane dived; we saw the wings shudder as the rockets were released. We hung on with our bare hands clutching the soil. My comrade at my side became a messy gore of rags. In front of me was the company dispatch rider with no legs. A man came running out of the dust and smoke, total bewilderment on his face.

Major Whittle has written the following account of the attack:

We reorganised in the area known as Horseshoe Wood to the west of Éterville. The information concerning the 7th Hampshires was very vague, and it was not certain whether some of them were still fighting in or near Maltot. At 1620 hrs the attack began. We still had our squadron of Churchill tanks in support, but owing to the position of the 7th Hampshires there was no artillery support initially. The ground was flattish, and the fields were filled with high standing corn; I remember moving forward in my carrier with the corn almost level with the sides, and wishing it was much higher! Approaching the village, we came under very heavy machine-gun and anti-tank-gun fire; the enemy had a large number of tanks and self-propelled guns dug in in concealed positions in the orchards and woods surrounding the village. We suffered heavy casualties and many of our tanks were knocked out. As far as I know, all our Anti-Tank platoon guns were destroyed before they had a chance to go into action. The rifle companies and Carrier Platoon all reached their objective, and began to consolidate, by 1645 hrs.

The divisional history records that:

Lieutenant-Colonel H.E. Cowie, the CO, arrived at the HQ of 7th Hampshires on the outskirts of the village just behind his leading companies. Too late he learnt that what remained of 7th Hampshires were being withdrawn. Meanwhile his two leading companies, expecting to take over from the Hampshires, advanced straight into the enemy position and were surrounded. The troop of S.P. guns with the battalion was quickly knocked out. Enemy tanks worked round to the rear of the remainder of the battalion, which lay out in the fields, exposed to fire from every direction. The position had become desperate…

The enemy action had split the battalion into isolated groups. The headquarters remained on the northern outskirts of the village, where it dug in and was joined by men who had lost contact. The rifle companies pushed on, harassed by enemy fire. Fighting amongst the gardens and houses they lost contact with each other and with Battalion Headquarters. Lance-Corporal Portway was with one of those groups moving through the battered and burning village:

Most of the flames gave off no smoke at all. We could feel the heat as we climbed over the debris. We came to a large hole in the ground…As usual, no one knew where we were going or what we supposed to do. After the carnage in the fields no one felt particularly heroic.

Captain Hall's company took their objective and planted their totem:

> The other Companies suffered heavily. Then we were surrounded by Tiger tanks and one silly one came to about fifty yards of our totem and blew it to pieces. I gave no order but my chaps rushed in and the tank and its crew were dead in about three minutes.

By 1645 hrs most of the 4th Dorsets had reached Maltot and were attempting to consolidate defensive positions. But once again confused fighting resulted. Lance-Corporal Chris Portway, with the leading companies, describes the action at the edge of the village:

> We were in an empty tank pit sheltering from the mortar fire and sorting ourselves to continue, when we saw a coal scuttle helmeted head peer over the rim. But he was too slow and we got him with a single shot before he could stick grenade us... We burst out of the pit firing in all directions and headed for the nearest house. Clearing each house, we moved on until in one we were sorting out our remaining ammunition, when we heard movement upstairs. We listened and aimed shots through the ceiling above where we thought the Jerry was. We missed and he sent a shower of grenades down the stairs and holes in the floor. Fortunately no one was seriously wounded and we eventually got him.

Major Whittle continued:

> The next two or three hours were very unpleasant. We had failed to knock out the majority of the dug-in tanks, and in the partly wooded area they were very difficult to locate; the few Churchills remaining with us were withdrawn, and fighting was going on all the time. Battalion Headquarters lost contact with all the rifle companies, and eventually at 2030 hrs there was a small party, consisting of the CO, Battalion Headquarters, parts of 'B', 'C' and 'D' Companies, and the Carrier Platoon, dug in on the northern outskirts of the village. We were under heavy direct fire from several of the dug-in tanks. The 112th Field Regiment put down extremely accurate artillery support which helped us.

Ken Stovey, a member of 217 Battery (112th Field Regiment) which supported the 7th Hampshires, entered Maltot that day:

> It was like walking into a huge wasp's nest, with Germans, tanks, mortars and Nebelwerfers everywhere. Our carrier was on fire, so we used a number 19 radio set in a Churchill tank until that 'brewed up'. Major Penrose and Captain Cash each earned a MC for taking command of all artillery to create a ring of fire around our perimeter. The 4th Dorsets came to our aid, but were put in the same situation.

Private Frank Porter, of the battalion's Mortar Platoon recalls his involvement during the action:

> We were firing all day from the Odon Valley but I don't know what at. We only got the direction, the elevation and charge that we were to use. We didn't have the asbestos

gloves that we were supposed to have, so we used wetted sandbags to move the barrels that were so hot that the paint had burnt off. The mortars got so hot that there was a danger of the bombs exploding before they left the barrel.

For three hours the Dorsets hung on as platoons and sections fought their own cat and mouse battles with the SS-Panzer-Grenadiers, as the riflemen progressively lost contact with their Battalion, Company and even Platoon Headquarters. They were surrounded by enemy infantry and tanks concealed in the wooded areas, where they were difficult to locate. Control had been lost and Battalion Headquarters had failed to regain contact with any of the rifle companies. The battle had now reached a climax, five company commanders having been lost, there was some disorganisation. The position was helpless, Colonel Cowie was therefore given permission, at 2030 hrs, to withdraw what remained of his battalion and it was almost nine o'clock in the evening when the Commanding Officer gave the order to withdraw. Four hours after they entered the village, the remnants of the 4th Dorsets dug in on the northern outskirts of Maltot and were given permission to exfiltrate back towards Château de Fontaine and Éterville. However, the order failed to reach men fighting in the village; all of 'A' Company and most of the other three rifle companies were left behind. As the day declined the survivors collected in the area of the 5th Dorsets and the 7th Somersets around Château de Fontaine.

Sergeant Caines was with those who withdrew:

> The CO reluctantly gave the order to withdraw, and the CO, Battalion Headquarters, parts of 'B', 'C' and 'D' Companies, and the Carrier Platoon withdrew under extremely accurate support from 112th Field Regiment. We passed back through 7th Somersets and took up a position in the area of Horseshoe Wood. During the withdrawal I went back with RSM Drew to help bring in a private soldier who had had a foot blown right off, and who up till then had been hopping along on his rifle; he remained quite conscious and cheerful until we got him to an MO; only then did he pass out.

Capt. R.F. Hall also received the order to withdraw:

> We hung on there, under considerable fire, completely surrounded by Tiger tanks and our battalion (or what remained of it) was ordered to withdraw at 2030 hrs because we had suffered severe casualties so, just for fun, we killed two more Tigers on the way out and fortunately only suffered three or four casualties. We managed to kill the first of the Tigers by stuffing a very heavy angle iron into the tracks and stopping it and then smothering it, the other silly one stopped of its own accord and so we just smothered that one as well. To cover our withdrawal a barrage much heavier than El Alamein, the whole divisional artillery plus two AGRAs! [Army Group Royal Artillery] My general impression of the day was of horrendous noise, a lot of dirt and muck flying about, terrible sights of bodies here and there, German and our own, some of them whole (but dead of course) others in bits, bits of bodies lying around. There wasn't much smell except of high explosives, but a lot of dirt and muck and horrendous noise all the time from enemy fire and from our own fire going over. It was quite a sobering experience

but my lads stood up very well and having come back from Maltot we dug in and held a position at the bottom of the hill for the night. But at the end of the day there were only five officers and about eighty other ranks (mostly mine) remaining of 4th Dorsets.

Only a minority of the Dorsets got the message to withdraw. Lance-Corporal Portway and others from his platoon were among those who were not informed to move back:

> …the rattle of gunfire had gradually died away, leaving only a solitary rifle shot here and there. It was a strange silence, an eerie silence, an eerie sense of solitude. There were five of us in a ditch. We knew what had happened. The battalion had gone. We hadn't heard the order. There was only one thing to do. Wait for darkness and then try to get back… Then the artillery opened up again. This time it was different: the scream of shells and the village became a hell on earth. We were on the wrong end of our own artillery bombardment… Silence again; then voices – German voices. Would they pass by? Then I saw blood trickling down the shoulder of my jacket. The man next to me was dead. Guttural voices and exclamations. Three German soldiers stood above us. We lifted our hands in the air.

In driving both the Hampshires and the Dorsets out of Maltot, the Germans had eliminated a salient deep into their defences north of the Orne. They followed up their success, under the gathering darkness, with counter-attacks by elements of the 10th ('Frundsberg') and the 1st ('Liebstandarte') SS-Panzer-Divisions.

That morning when Lance-Corporal Butt had sounded the charge on his bugle, 500 men had risen to their feet and cheered. They had stormed Éterville with a panache that had taken the SS defenders by surprise. Now, fourteen hours later, only five officers and fewer than eighty men had come back. Many lay dead with the Hampshires in Maltot; many were wounded. A few got back during the night; others were taken prisoner. The survivors were shattered and exhausted.

After several anxious hours, the remnants of companies collected and established a defensive position along several hundred yards of front. Some men were without rifles or ammunition, and many had lost their equipment completely. Those without gathered from the wounded and the dead, so by nightfall almost every man possessed some sort of fighting iron. The Signals Officer informed 'Wally' Caines that the carrier with the bulk of the signals equipment had been destroyed by a shell. So there were no communications facilities in the battalion. Most of the wireless sets carried by the company signallers had been knocked out, or left behind in Maltot.

Major Whittle recalled:

> The attack on Maltot had accounted for the whole of 'A' Company, of which not one member returned, and for two-thirds of the other three companies. Major Upton, Major Conner and Major Dawson, commanding 'A', 'C' and 'D' Companies respectively, were all missing. It was subsequently learned that a large number of the missing were taken prisoner during the night. Battalion strength that night was five officers including the CO and less than eighty ORs, excluding LOBs and echelons. Later we

were reinforced by small parties from several different regiments; a large contingent from the Essex Regiment, including some officers who went 'en bloc' to form a completely new 'A' Company. Captain Roper and Captain Letson were both promoted to Major and took over 'C' and 'D' Coys. I took over 'S' Company.

The 4th Dorsets had forty-eight members of the battalion killed in action on 10 July and nearly 300 wounded or taken prisoner. Geoff Cleal was a member of a burial party involving eleven members of the battalion. His task was to remove identification, pay books and personal belongings. 'This was a harrowing task. I stuffed the belongings in my pockets and haversack'. CSM Symes, who collected the remains of 'D' Company summed up the situation, 'A lot of brave men came out of Maltot and a lot were left behind'. Like many other infantry battalions, the 4th Dorsets suffered the worst casualties of the whole North-West Europe campaign in their first full scale action. The Territorial heart of the brigade, built up over years of pre-war service and five years of home defence and training, was ripped out in a single day's battle. After the battle, on and around Hill 112, all battalions of the 43rd Division required reinforcements, which in effect, produced new battalions. In common with many other divisions, the character of the units under command of 43rd Wessex Division changed forever.

Over 400 men of the 43rd Wessex Division were killed or died of wounds during Operation Jupiter on 10 and 11 July – about 28 per cent of the divisions total fatalities in the Normandy campaign in little over a thirty-six hour period. During Jupiter, the 130th Brigade were the worst affected with 179 fatalities, almost evenly spread between the three infantry battalions, then the 129th Brigade with 124 deaths, and the 214th Brigade with eighty-two – sixty-nine of which were from the 5th DCLI – the highest loss by any British battalion in a single action in Normandy, D-Day included. The 7th Hampshires also lost more than sixty men killed in Jupiter.

'Wally' Caines, reflecting on the previous twenty-four hours, wrote:

We spent the night of 10/11 July in a position just forward of Horseshoe Wood. As dawn broke (on the 11th) every man stood to in his newly dug slit trench, ready to deal with the expected assault from the enemy. It was considered that Jerry had possibly reorganised his troops during the night and would assault in the morning. All of us were cold as stones, extremely worn out and dog tired... I myself felt fit to drop, it had been a terrible twenty-four hours, something I will never forget as long as I live, seeing men fall, and hearing the wounded cry and moan with pain as they were evacuated. I could never express in my own words the horror experienced on this day.

But the expected attack did not come, and at 0530 hrs on the 11th the battalion again moved forward to take up a position halfway between Fontaine and Maltot, the village having been recaptured by the Germans, and remained there until relieved by the 5th Dorsets in the evening, when it went to reorganise in the area of Colleville, north of the River Odon. It spent three days re-equipping at Colleville, which proved to be smack in the middle of a gun area, where they were continually catching some of the counter-battery fire. There were several casualties, two of whom were the MO and the Padre, who were both wounded.

'Wally' Caines wrote in his journal:

> 11 July. At noon the IO Lt Andrews saw Jerries forming up in a cornfield 800 yards away with a few tanks behind them. He stood on top of the Battery Commander's scout car directing the gunner officer on the position of the enemy. We thanked God for this, as within a few minutes down came our murderous artillery barrage crashing amongst the Jerries in the cornfield. Two enemy tanks went up in smoke and flames. The artillery came to the rescue again. Relieved by 5th Dorsets at 1800 hrs we had to march back seven miles to Colleville rest area. It was a pitiful sight to see the thin column of marching troops, none of us dressed alike. Several padres met us with cheery smiles, giving us cigarettes, chocolate and sweets.

> 12 July. Hot meal, went to sleep, all had a good wash down. Kits of deceased personnel had to be unloaded from the rear echelon vehicles. Tears came to my eyes as I looked through photographs of wives and girlfriends belonging to the boys I had known so well.

> 14 July. Some 300 reinforcements arrived. Battalion formed into strong companies making the total strength about 400, remaining 200 newly joined fighting troops were told to remain in the field for the day. Colonel Cowie was to leave us to join another part of the Army for duty.

The Battalion War Diary records that between the 12 and 13 July, 350 replacement Other Ranks and seven Officers were sent from 33 RHU (Reinforcement Holding Unit) to help re-establish the unit's strength following the heavy fighting at Éterville and Maltot. Evidence, if evidence were needed, that the 4th Dorsets first major engagement had taken a heavy toll of those original members of the battalion.

Major Whittle wrote:

> At 2315 hrs on the 14th the Battalion, now commanded by Lieutenant-Colonel L.J. Wood returned to Maltot, relieving the 1st Worcesters in the line about one mile to the north-west of the village. We moved into a defensive position overlooking Maltot, in the area of the Château de Fontaine, to the south-west of Éterville. The position was on a forward slope, and we were continually being mortared and shelled; no movement was possible during daylight, and supplies and ammunition were brought up each night. There were numerous dead cattle in the fields and many dead Germans in the hedges, and the stench was foul.

Gunner Ken Stovey re-entered Maltot some days after the battle to a scene that he considered worse than the battle itself:

> Hampshires, 4th and 5th Dorsets and Germans lay where they fell all mingled together. The smell was horrendous with swarms of flies and wasps. There were some graves and on one we managed to identify a protractor laying on top of a grave as belonging to Lt Blincow.

Lieutenant Joseph Sydney Blincow, of the 112th Field Artillery, was killed on 10 July and was reburied in Banneville-La-Campagne War Cemetery after the hostilities were over. Maltot was a dreadful spectacle, the streets and fields were still strewn with the dead (Dorsets and Hampshires who had fallen on 10 July) and lay in heaps around slit trenches with hardly any more than the turf removed. The houses were shattered, roads cratered and full of debris; everywhere the sickly smell of death and destruction hung heavily upon the ruins.

The battalion remained outside of Maltot until the 18th and had a particularly unpleasant time, as enemy mortaring and shelling were constant, with a large number of casualties. One mortar exploded in the Battalion Headquarters, wounding the IO and the CO (Lieutenant-Colonel Wood) who were both admitted to the 20th General Hospital, Bayeux. Colonel Wood returned a few days later and in the meantime the second-in-command, Major Tilly, from the 5th Dorsets, was promoted and assumed command. At 2200 hrs the same day the battalion was obliged to take up a new position 300yds to the rear, where it remained until the 26th. During this period the battalion witnessed a huge daylight bomber force putting down a 'carpet' about one mile in front of their positions; it was an awe-inspiring sight. During this period a prisoner was taken who turned out to be a German Pay Corps NCO, and had, in a heavy leather briefcase, a considerable sum of money in French francs. He was apparently making the rounds of the forward positions, and had ventured a little too far forward. As a result of his indiscretion more than 250,000 francs went to the regimental prisoner-of-war fund. In the early hours of the 21st two more prisoners were

A British Churchill tank in the shattered village of Maltot, 26 July 1944. (Imperial War Museum B 8051)

brought to the Battalion Headquarters by 'B' Company, being identified as members of the 10.SS-Panzer-Division ('Frundsberg'), one of whom spoke very good English and provided valuable information, which was then passed on to division.

Major Whittle had a narrow escape, but not so his fellow trench occupant:

> One night (24th) an enemy plane dropped a bomb about thirty yards from 'S' Company Headquarters, and the new Anti-Tank Platoon commander, who was with me in my trench, was hit in the chest; he had arrived only about thirty minutes earlier.

Lance-Corporal Frederick Bocock, aged thirty-one years, was killed during the raid.

It was without regret that the Wessex Division handed over the battle-scarred slopes of Hill 112 and the stinking ruins of Maltot to 53rd (Welsh) Division on 25 July. Except for the capture of Éterville, which deserves to rank high in the annals of the Regiment, and the subsequent heavy fighting at Maltot, the 4th Dorsets played no part in the fighting for Caen, and on the afternoon of 26 July moved into the rest area of Condé-sur-Seulles, about six miles south-east of Bayeux. On its arrival the battalion received its first hot meal for many days, as all the time it had been in the Fontaine-Maltot sector each man had been obliged to cook for himself on a Tommy cooker; a compact, portable, solidified-alcohol fuelled stove. 'Wally' Caines reflected:

> I shall never forget the sight the men looked when they returned, dirty, muddy clothes, and hardly a man had shaved in eight days, but they were all on top form, they arrived singing popular songs, and all had the usual wisecrack.

The three days at Condé were mainly spent in cleaning up, re-equipping and reorganising; the Divisional Commander visited the brigade and congratulated it on its performance, and there was a certain amount of recreation: an ENSA (Entertainments National Service Association) show visited the camp, and the men were given an opportunity of visiting Bayeux.

Brigadier Essame of the 214th Brigade provides an enlightening description of the Divisional rest area:

> The rest area had been so rapidly overrun on D-Day that much of the corn stood undamaged and ripening in the fields. The Norman countryside had an English air. The churches, village green and big solid farms had their counterparts across the Channel in the West Country. It was pleasant to bivouac in the shade of the apple-trees away from the din of the battlefield and the all-pervading dust and traffic of the bridgehead, or to visit the mobile bath unit established by the RAOC on the River Seulles and enjoy the luxury of a bath and clean underwear. Bayeux, choked with the apparently necessary military population which makes up the tail of an army, offered few attractions. For the administrative staffs, the services and the quartermasters and transport officers, this brief respite provided the opportunity to re-equip their units. So untiring and successful were their efforts that when unexpected orders to move reached units during the night of 28th/29th July, the Division was able to march in an entirely new direction on the following day reinforced to full strength and once more ready for battle.

# Chapter 7

# La Bigne

On 27 July, General Montgomery ordered the British Second Army to regroup and strike south from Caumont (l'Evente) on the 30th to capture Mont Pinçon (as vital a hill as 112) at 1,200ft the highest point in Normandy. During the night of the 28th orders were sent out from Divisional Headquarters for an 'O' Group at 0800 hrs on the following morning. When this assembled, Major-General Thomas revealed that the Wyverns were to be part of XXX Corps (Lieutenant-General Gerard Bucknall), which included the 50th (Northumbrian) Infantry Division, the 7th Armoured, the 56th Infantry Brigade and the 8th Armoured Brigade.

The plan for Operation Bluecoat was for XXX Corps to push south-east, to the line Villers-Bocage – Aunay-sur-Odon, while VIII Corps, in a wider sweep on its right, swung down to the general area Saint-Martin-des-Besaces – Le Bény-Bocage – Forêt l'Éveque, and on to the triangle formed by Vire, Tinchebray and Condé-sur-Noireau. Compared with the country around Caen, the scene change was striking. The whole area was more hilly and wooded than the country in the bridgehead and the principal feature was a series of hills running south-east between Le Bény-Bocage and Aunay-sur-Odon. Several of the hills were over 1,000ft high.

Operation Bluecoat was fought in progressively more hilly country, broken by streams flowing through steep-sided valleys. The streams ran in all directions, their bridges too fragile to carry tanks or heavy vehicles. There were few towns of any size and most of the population lived in small villages or farmsteads. The hills were covered with thick woodland while the characteristic dairy farms and orchards of the region occupied the valleys and slopes. The small fields and innumerable, often sunken, side roads were lined with banked hedgerows and ditches, frequently with a line of tall close-growing tress in addition. These narrow, sunken lanes, some as deep as 20ft, linked together the many small villages and farms. The lanes were too narrow for vehicles and a serious obstacle to cross-country movement. In addition, they provided the enemy with ready-made trenches. Stone walls enclosed the orchards and the stone buildings and narrow streets of the villages completed a countryside ideal for defenders. For the first time the Wyverns were venturing into genuine *bocage* country – 'la Suisse Normande'. It was the most rugged part of the *bocage* and the Germans were strongly entrenched on the slopes and ridges.

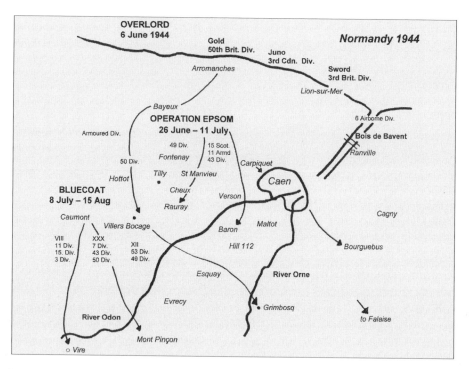

The progress of the 43rd Wessex Division through Normandy in 1944, from Arromanches to Maltot and Hill 112, and Operation Bluecoat.

For XXX Corps, Operation Bluecoat began at 0600 hrs on 30 July. 43rd Division was to secure the hill feature about Point 361, at the western end of the Mont Pinçon ridge, to the west of Jurques, while the 50th Division on its left was to secure the high ground west and north-west of Villers-Bocage. In the centre of the Bluecoat attack, 43rd Division's first task was to force through enemy positions at Briquessard and north of Cahagnes and advance via Saint-Pierre-du-Fresne to seize Bois du Homme – the high ground west and south-west of Jurques. At the same time they were to protect the eastern flank of XXX Corps by seizing and holding the La Bigne feature. Finally, they were to swing east and capture the high ground at Ondefontaine as a base for further deep reconnaissance in easterly and south-easterly directions. The 130th Brigade, augmented by the 4th Somerset Light Infantry, was to lead the assault.

It was intended that the battalion should rest for ten days at Condé-sur-Seulles, but events made that impossible. The capture of the Faubourg de Vaucelles, the part of Caen south of the River Orne, completed the breakthrough along the whole of the Allied line, and on 29 July the 4th Dorsets left Condé for the area of Couvigny-le-Repas, about two miles north-east of Caumont, where they arrived in the late afternoon. With the 5th Dorsets on its left, the battalion was ordered to attack the hamlet of La Londe with a squadron of tanks under command and full artillery support and, if successful, to push on to Cahagnes. At 0920 hrs on the 30th, the battalion moved up to the start line, but at 1000 hrs the attack was postponed and the battalion waited all day in position for it to begin, suffering from constant mortaring and a fair amount of shelling. At 1800 hrs the attack was cancelled and the 7th Hampshires were ordered to attack La Londe from the flank, while the 4th Dorsets concentrated for the night some 400yds behind the start line.

During the night orders were received to clear the ground in front of the 5th Dorsets, whose progress was impeded by a large number of the enemy, and at 0500 hrs on the 31st the 4th Dorsets moved forward to Montmirel, about one mile east of Caumont, had breakfast and dug in. The CO decided to move round by the west and to make the attack due east, thus moving across the front of the 5th Dorsets on the left, the right being protected by the 7th Hampshires, who had captured La Londe and advanced beyond it. At 0900 hrs patrols of 'A' Company, commanded by Major Grafton, were sent south to the orchards surrounding La Londe, and at 1500 hrs the main body of the battalion started the attack from Montmirel. It went exceptionally well and in about four hours the objective was taken, as well as eighty-seven prisoners, for the cost of half a dozen casualties. The Pioneer Platoon under Sergeant Blandemer did excellent work in clearing anti-personnel minefields. The battalion was immediately ordered to swing south to capture Point 174 on the ridge south-east of Caumont, and in the heat of a gruelling afternoon it moved forward to its new objective, which it captured without opposition. Here it dug in for the night, which was remarkable for the fact that no firing of any sort took place and that the quietness was uncanny. Patrols were sent forward all night long and returned with a few prisoners. The battalion stayed in its new position throughout 1 August, when mortaring was fairly constant.

'Wally' Caines observed:

> 1 August. The weather was blisteringly hot, shirt sleeve order. Several dead animals, victims of the shelling, lay around the whole area we were occupying... The stink was terrible, especially during the night after a long hot day; the dead animals were literally running with maggots and flies. At 2100 hrs Lieutenant-Colonel G. Tilly succeeded the unfortunate Lieutenant-Colonel Wood.

However, the Battalion's War Diary records that it was on 2 August that Major Tilly (second-in-command) assumed command of the battalion in the absence of the CO who had returned to 'B' Echelon for a rest.

The Germans responded to the Allied advance and on 1 August a Korps order went out to the divisions with the following content:

> II.SS-Panzer-Korps with subordinated 9th and 10th SS-Panzer-Divisions and 21.Panzer-Division to clear out, by counter-attack of the 10.SS-Panzer-Division, the enemy penetration at Coulvain and, with the 21.Panzer-Division and 9.SS-Panzer-Division, close the gap between the LXXIV. Armeekorps and the east wing of the 7. Armee.

In order to carry out the detailed Korps order, the 10.SS-Panzer-Division ('Frundsberg') immediately set off with all available units to the Aunay-sur-Odon – Ondefontaine sector. During the afternoon of 1 August a Kampfgruppe (battle group) of the 10.SS-Panzer-Division, under the leadership of SS-Obersturmbannführer Otto Paetsch, was on the march to the hard-pressed frontal sector at Aunay-sur-Odon.

First off was SS-Sturmbannführer Heinrich Brinkmann's Reconnaissance Battalion, SS-Panzer-Aufklärungs-Abteilung 10 (SS-Pz.AA.10) with the mission of reconnaissance and establishment of contact with the units of the 326.Infantry Division that were still holding out. The patrols to the west and south-west of Aunay-sur-Odon were to be carried out by their armoured 1st and 2nd Panzer-Spähwagen Kompanies. Brinkmann's unit was followed by SS-Sturmbannführer Leo Reinhold's II. Bataillon of SS-Panzer-Regiment 10 and a company of SS-Panzer-Pionier-Batallion 10. Just before 2200 hrs Kampfgruppe Paetsch reached Aunay-sur-Odon. The route march came to a halt in the bomb-destroyed Aunay, where the 3rd Pionier-Kompanie was set to clear the highway through the village.

British divisional plans had been for Bois du Homme to be secured and le Mesnil-Auzouf captured before continuing to Ondefontaine. However, with 129th Brigade fully committed on the slopes of Bois du Homme, an immediate advance on Ondefontaine was required if 43rd Division was to make more rapid progress. That evening the Commanding Officer was informed that the division was to make a break-out on the road Caumont – Cahagnes – Jurques – Ondefontaine; the 130th Brigade was to move that night, and the 4th Dorsets were to lead the attack with a squadron of Sherman tanks, a section of RE (Royal Engineers), a platoon of anti-tank guns and a platoon of medium machine guns under command. Their task was to seize Jurques, La Bigne and Ondefontaine; the capture of La Bigne was essential, but if the battalion suffered heavy casualties there, another battalion would pass through to take Ondefontaine. It was anticipated that the battalion would cover twenty miles without meeting any enemy, an estimate that turned out to be incorrect.

In the meanwhile, SS-Obersturmbannführer Paetsch discussed the situation with LXXIV.Armeekorps at the command post in the Château de Courvaudon, five kilo-metres east of Aunay-sur-Odon. Paetsch consequently decided to secure the area of Aunay-sur-Odon – Ondefontaine in order to conceal the advance of follow-ing units of the 10.SS-Panzer-Division and to advance with partial forces during the night as far as the crisis at Jurques – Bremoy. SS-Obersturmbannführer Rudolf Harmstorf's 1st Panzerspähkompanie was ordered to reconnoitre the combat lines south of Caumont between Coulvain and Jurques to establish how far the enemy had penetrated. SS-Sturmbannführer Brinkmann's Aufklärungs-Abteilung had, in the meantime, wormed its way through the destruction at Aunay-sur-Odon and advanced towards Ondefontaine. The main body of Kampfgruppe Paetsch closed up. Brinkmann's Abteilung drove further along the route Ondefontaine – La Bigne and was fired on by the enemy in the Bois de Buron. The Abteilung took up positions one kilometre east of La Bigne. The II./SS-Panzer-Regiment 10 had also marched on, advancing to the left of the Aufklärungs-Abteilung as far as the Caen –Vire high-way, and went into position two kilometres south of Jurques after contact with the enemy.

The 4th Dorsets and its supporting arms concentrated at 2330 hrs on 1 August; tanks of B Squadron Sherwood Rangers in the van. As the Dorsets formed up along the side of the road, enemy aircraft dropped parachute flares and illuminated the area completely, following up with anti-personnel bombs, but were well off their target. At 0115 hrs on the 2nd the battalion moved off south-westwards at a steady pace, the

Carrier Platoon leading. Captain Hall, by now a Company Commander, was leading his company with a Bren gun carrier section down a road in the dark:

> All went well until we came to a place called Cahagnes, where on the crossroads we saw somebody with a red lamp. We stopped and myself, and Mike Whittle, the commander of the Bren gun carrier section, wandered forward to see what was going on. We found a military policeman with a red hurricane lamp. We asked him what he was doing there, to which he responded, 'I'm directing the traffic, and you're supposed to go down that way!' It transpired that he had been told to stand there and direct the traffic but had arrived far too early before even we had arrived. We carried on down the road towards Mont Pinçon and when we got to a village called Jurques we started to catch up with the Germans and came across mines on the road and a few pockets of resistance which we managed to clear up fairly successfully.

At 0915 hrs the 4th Dorsets 'A' Company, the leading company, was within half a mile of Jurques and encountered mines. The road was heavily cratered and while searching for mines a machine gun opened up. Patrols pushed forward and met opposition for the first time. 'Wally' Caines recalls, 'A few fanatics were holding out in the village itself. These fools were quickly dealt with, and were no more'. At this point the Adjutant, Captain Goddard, in trying to catch up with the column, took a different route and entered Jurques in front of 'A' Company. Major Whittle recollects:

> We heard an explosion and pushed forward, and halfway between Jurques and La Bigne we found the Adjutant's scout car blown up on a mine. Captain Goddard had been killed outright, and Lieutenant Bogan, the Signal Officer, was badly burned on the face and hands.

Between Jurques and La Bigne the country was hilly and very close, and afforded excellent positions for the Germans to delay the advance from the front and flanks. The road was mined, and while the Sappers and the battalion Pioneers were clearing it, the column was engaged by fire from the flank. The battalion passed through Jurques fairly easily and 'A' Company moved on up the hill, but on reaching the top, a few hundred yards from La Bigne, it came under very heavy fire and suffered heavy casualties.

Captain Hall wrote:

> By the morning of 2 August we had reached a place called La Bigne where there was a fork in the road. We had to take the right-hand turning and my forward platoon move up there. They immediately came under very heavy fire from the enemy and they were completely wiped out. My whole Company was pinned to the ground by mortar, very heavy machine gun fire and everybody was a little scared.

The battalion, up against positions of 3. (Leichte-Panzer-Aufklärungs) Kompanie of SS-Pz.AA.10, made another attempt to go forward, and the CO decided to put in two more companies, supported by tanks, as soon as the mines were cleared. The Pioneer

Platoon and the Sappers worked splendidly; the attack was not delayed, and by 1600 hrs La Bigne was captured and mopping-up operations were completed.

The diary of Sergeant Caines recalls the action:

> 2 August. The advance started somewhere in the region of 0015 hrs and carried on heading south towards the village of Jurques. It was a terrible night; troops were lifted on tanks, continuously dropping off to sleep. I was leading the column in a carrier driven by Private Brake. It was pitch dark and no one knew when the first pocket of resistance would be met, or whether we would be ambushed. I was as usual riding a motor cycle behind the second company. The Signals scout car travelling behind the leading company went off course, and was blown up on a mine, killing the Adjutant Captain Goddard and the control operator Corporal Penny; the Signal Officer had escaped but was badly burnt on the face and hands. Brigade and battalion control sets were knocked out. As we left the battered town we were faced with a hell of a resistance; Jerry then opened up with all he had, self-propelled guns and Spandaus. Several tanks were knocked out by carefully concealed anti-tank guns. Major Letson 'D' Coy was badly wounded, and also several sergeants and other NCOs. After heavy fighting we succeeded in capturing La Bigne, some two miles south of Jurques, but the battalion suffered numerous casualties again and were feeling worse for wear. All night long men dug and reinforced positions, while signallers were kept working on the endless task of getting a line through.

The German view of the day's events reveal that reconnaissance in all directions by the II./SS-Panzer-Regiment 10 showed that, in the early hours of 2 August, the

The small village of La Bigne, 11 September 1945, site of the battalion's action on 3 August 1944. Private John Paradise, of the 4th Dorsets, photographed the gaping hole left in the barn wall by a German shell.

British had penetrated in unknown strength as far as Pitot, Sauques, La Bigne and on to Hill 188, one kilometre south of Sauques. The patrol's advance during the night had stumbled across the British, the clashes which followed favouring the 'Tommies'. With weak forces, and without the power to orchestrate a true front line, Paetsch decided to set up his units in a series of defensive points, situated between Pied du Bois – south of La Bigne – Hill 301, taking advantage of the shape of the landscape. The importance of the height of Hill 301 became apparent at daybreak since the view opened up over the Odon valley and Jurques. In view of the enemy advance, the German reconnaissance reported that, 'the principal line of combat goes as far as Saint-Georges-d'Aunay – La Bigne – Hill 301 – Hill 321.

The 3. (Leichte-Panzer-Aufklärungs) Kompanie of SS-Pz.AA.10, under the command of SS-Obersturmführer Gerhard Hinze, was engaged on the road from Villers-Bocage to Vire in order to cover the left flank, with the bulk of the Aufklärungs-Abteilung occupying a position one kilometre east of La Bigne. This hastily-assembled blockade was enough to block the British advance during daylight on 2 August; only La Bigne was taken, by the 43rd Wessex Division. The 4th Dorsets were nevertheless obliged to retake the village two more times in the afternoon. The battalion, which distinguished itself three weeks earlier by taking Éterville before grinding to a halt outside Maltot suffered heavy losses during this engagement. The taking of the village was made very difficult by the Sturmgeschütze (self-propelled assault guns) of the II./SS-Panzer-Regiment 10 putting up 'a hell of a struggle'. This success was nevertheless very important, as it took an excellent defensive position dominating the Odon valley out of German hands. After that, the English division could aspire to their objective: a rapid occupation of Ondefontaine.

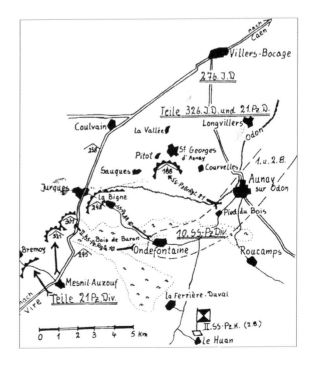

Commitment of the 10. SS-Panzer-Division at Aunay-sur-Odon, 2 August 1944 from the history of the 9th and 10th SS-Panzer-Divisions.

The Germans faced an important crisis during the afternoon of 2 August when some twenty British tanks pushed as far as Pitot and Hill 188, advancing from the hamlet of Sauques. This attack at the point of contact between the 74th Armee Korps and the II.SS-Panzer-Korps broke the links between the 326. Infantry Division and the 10.SS-Panzer-Division. This situation was especially critical as it was the last place where it is possible to anchor a solid defence to protect Aunay-sur-Odon, less than five kilometres away. That afternoon the II.SS-Panzer-Korps established its command post at Le Huan, where Oberführer Heinz Harmel decided on an attack on the British spearhead at Saint-Georges-d'Aunay from the area of Ondefontaine. SS-Obersturmbannführer Paetsch thus received the order to re-establish contact, come what may, with the neighbouring unit. One of the two regiments of Werfer-Brigade 8, whose multiple mortars had been used at Hill 112, was given the assignment to move towards this pressure point. As ordered, the 10.SS-Panzer-Division ('Frundsberg'), who had arrived late afternoon, moved out of the assembly position of Ondefontaine – Aunay to attack to the north-west on the morning of 3 August. Following concentrated fire strikes from the SS-Panzer-Artillerie-Regiment 10 on Hill 188, and on the village of La Bigne, the attack began. At full strength, the SS-Panzer-Artillerie-Regiment 10, commanded by SS-Standartenführer Hans Sander, had a complement of twelve Wespe self-propelled guns, six Hummel self-propelled howitzers, twelve 10.5cm light field pieces, twelve 15cm heavy field howitzers and four 10cm K18 Kanone (Cannon). Coinciding with the attack of the reinforced SS-Panzer-Regiment 21, under the command of SS-Obersturmbannführer Wilhelm Schulze, on Hill 188, an attack by Kampfgruppe Paetsch with SS-Pz.AA.10 and units of the II./SS-Panzer-Regiment 10 hit La Bigne. This attack was soon met by a British counter-attack. Kampfgruppe Paetsch went over to the defence before La Bigne and, simultaneously with another unit, defended against the enemy attack directed at Hill 301.

In the early hours of 2 August the 43rd Division had started from the Bois du Homme and, overcoming a number of attacks by small battle groups, had advanced some three miles through difficult country, driving the 21st Panzer-Division troops out of Jurques and capturing Hill 301, two miles to the south. Next day their progress was held up in stubborn fighting with newly-arrived troops of the 10.SS-Panzer-Division. The division was once more up against determined and well-organised opposition on ground which gave every advantage to the enemy.

The battalion's patrols found the enemy, in strength, was holding the woods beyond La Bigne and in Ondefontaine, so spent the late afternoon of the 2nd consolidating its position, and was mortared incessantly during the night and the following morning. During the evening of the 2nd, the 5th Dorsets were ordered to pass through and occupy Ondefontaine; they spent the whole of the 3rd trying to get through the thick wood where the road ran, but were frustrated by fierce resistance from well-hidden machine guns and tanks, and at 1400 hrs on the 3rd the 4th Dorsets (now commanded by Lieutenant-Colonel G. Tilly, since Lieutenant-Colonel L.J. Wood, who was still feeling the effect of his head wound, had again been evacuated the day before) attacked southwards from La Bigne. Their intention was to clear the woods west and south of Ondefontaine and to occupy the village. They ran into heavy fire

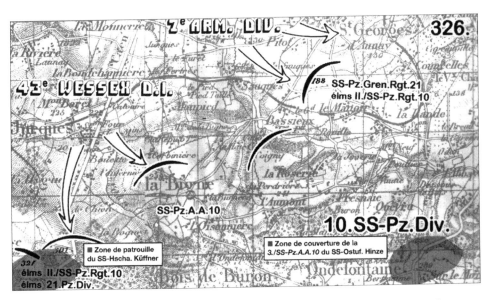

The situation in the La Bigne area, the evening of 3 August 1944, from the history of SS-Panzer-Aufklärungs-Abteilung 10.

and suffered severe casualties, but the objective was gained. At 1615 hrs the enemy counter-attacked, but this was beaten off in a couple of hours, and the battalion took up its original position for the night, during which it was heavily mortared and shelled.

Sergeant 'Wally' Caines wrote in his diary:

3 August. 'O' group to attack Ondefontaine 2½ miles ahead. 1330 hrs attack commenced. Forward troops left their trenches only to meet stiff enemy resistance. They were cut down like flies – every man pinned to the ground as all round Spandaus fired murderously. There was no hope of advancing. Our artillery plastered the Jerries. The attack kept up for about an hour then it was decided to withdraw to the original position. Our casualties were very heavy and many men still lay wounded amongst the dead in the cornfield. Some managed to crawl back to safety, others laid up until dark whilst a few remained to die of their wounds where they fell.

Particularly lethal were the rockets fired from the six-barrelled Nebelwerfers. The firepower was impressive: firing six 150mm projectiles in as many seconds. The ammunition was known as Wurfgranate 41 (German for 'rocket grenade'). The accuracy was not so good though; only half of the missiles hit a 130 by 180 metres rectangle around the aimed point (the dispersion), and whilst the explosive head was modest (less than 3kg), the morale outcome was considerable. Nebelwerfer fire was infinitely worse when it descended on those unprotected by any overhead shelter, since the fragmentation effect of these bombs was great. Neillands provides an interesting account of 'Moaning Minnies', as the electronically-ignited rockets were nicknamed:

The shelling was pretty horrendous and it was far more dangerous in wooded areas when the shells detonated above the branches and shrapnel cascaded downwards. Air bursts exploded about six feet from the ground and sprayed shrapnel like an umbrella.

This is how Brigadier Essame of the 214th Brigade, at the 'receiving-end' recalled his baptism by this kind of fire:

A few seconds later a howling and wailing grew until it filled the sky, rising in pitch as it approached, and ending in a series of shattering explosions all round. There was a pause. Then more squeals, the same horrible wail, and another batch of thirty-six bombs exploded astride us, so that the blast came first from one side, then from the other, then from both.

The small size and light impact of it's weaponry made the Nebelwerfer practically useless against armoured targets such as tanks and personnel carriers, but the dense and sustained penetration of its multiple rockets made it extraordinarily lethal when used against unarmoured enemy infantry. After the crew had loaded and aimed the launcher, they would take cover a few metres away and fire the Nebelwerfer by an electric wire. After firing, however, a long streak of smoke could be seen for some distance, making the Nebelwerfer an easy target for coun-

Nebelwerfer 41: the six-barrelled rocket launcher, known to the allied soldiers as 'Moaning Minnies'; often referred to incorrectly as a 'six-barrelled mortar'.

ter-artillery fire. It was therefore imperative to reposition the Nebelwerfer as soon as possible after firing.

Except for a few rocket artillery units in the 1.SS and 12.SS-Panzer-Divisions and the Army's 21.Panzer-Division, all Nebelwerfer were in non-divisional units; three Werfer-Brigaden and one Werfer-Regiment together comprised twenty-one battalions plus a few extra batteries. A battalion with 150mm Nebelwerfers had eighteen launchers, each with six barrels. Within seconds, a battalion could fire 108 150mm rockets. The most likely unit supporting SS-Pz.AA.10 with Nebelwerfer fire on 3 August was Werfer-Brigade 8 – comprising Werfer-Lehr-Regiment 1 and Schweres-Werfer-Regiment 2, both armed with 150mm and 210mm werfers, even though SS-Werfer-Abteilung 102 was also in the area. Their Tageskriegbuch (War Diary) records that on 1 August the unit was 'still attached to Werfer-Brigade 8' in the area of Maisoncelles-Pelvey – Courqueret, approximately nine miles to the north-east of La Bigne, but by 3 August the unit had moved to Montchamp, about 10 miles south of La Bigne, supporting an attack by Panzer-Kampfgruppe Meyer.

Bert's role in the battalion was as Company Runner, a responsible job, conveying the requests and instructions of the Company Commander. Responsibilities included taking verbal messages (not written messages), and instructing men to move up if required during action. It was whilst carrying out these duties that he was seriously wounded:

The Nebelwerfer 41 was capable of firing six 75lb 150mm projectiles in as many seconds, over a range of 6,800 metres (about 4.2 miles); a full salvo spread over a period of 10 seconds.

The morning of 3 August we were going into the attack and I was Company Runner. We had started to advance when the Company Commander said to me, 'Where is No. 2 Platoon?' I replied, 'Still in the trenches Sir', and I was told that they should be in the line of advance. I went back to where they were in their slit trenches where I stood facing them and gave them the Company Commander's orders. All the time the Germans were laying down a mortar barrage of six-barrelled mortars which fire six bombs in succession and were called 'moaning minnies', because they made a screaming noise as they were fired. They had a very demoralising effect on us and were very frightening. One bomb dropped behind me and knocked me out and when I regained consciousness I had been wounded in the back and was bleeding rather badly. All the men in 2 Platoon who were in the trenches and took the full force of the blast in their faces were dead.

When he came to, Bert said a little prayer to himself:

Please God, I don't mind dying, but please don't let me die in a foreign field.

Whilst lying on the ground wounded, waiting for stretcher-bearers, Bert put his 'tin hat' over his face in order to protect himself from the mortar shells that were still coming down! As he lay on the ground his outstretched hand found a jerrycan nearby containing liquid. Thinking it was water he took a swig, only to discover what he thought was Calvados, an apple brandy that is a speciality of Normandy. It is possible that Bert was mistaken and it was actually cider that he drank. One unit in the division, the 43rd Reconnaissance Regiment, issued an order, recorded in the War Diary for 31 July 1944, stating that, 'Water jerrycans are not to be used for cider', presumably because it was common practice.

After some time the stretcher-bearers, who were very hard pressed, picked me up and took me back to the medical post where they gave me emergency treatment for my wounds. All the time this was happening the mortar barrage continued and at one stage the medic Corporal Puddy covered me with his body to protect me from further injury. I later learned that he too had been killed.

Lance-Corporal William Anthony Malcolm Puddy, the son of William and Alice Puddy, of Parkstone, Dorset, was killed on 15 August 1944, aged twenty-seven years, and is buried in Tilly-sur-Seulles War Cemetery, Normandy.

After he had been tended by Lance-Corporal Puddy, Bert was taken to No. 10 Casualty Clearing Station (CCS), located at Juaye-Mondaye, five miles south of Bayeux and about twenty miles from La Bigne, being diagnosed with 'multiple mortar wounds back – penetrating chest'. The medical report of 12 September 1944 states he 'received shell wounds (mortar) at 1230 hrs'. 75 per cent of all wounds in Normandy were caused by mortars and shellfire. During the night of 2/3 August, No. 10 CCS received sixty-three battle casualties – all serious cases as 163rd Field Ambulance were categorizing and sending only those cases urgently needing operations. In order to deal with the influx of casualties two additional Field Surgical Units and one Field Transfusion Unit were sent to help, and with two surgical teams from

ORIGINAL

WAR DIARY
or
INTELLIGENCE SUMMARY.
(Erase heading not required).

Army Form C. 211°

A BN. DORSET REGT.

LT. COL. L. J. WOOD.

Instructions regarding War Diaries and Intelligence Summaries are contained in F.S. Regs., Part II. and the Staff Manual respectively. Title pages will be prepared in manuscript.

AUG 44

| Place | Date | Hour | Summary of Events and Information | Remarks and references to Appendices |
|---|---|---|---|---|
| 734581 | 1 | 0550 | 2 FWD O.P's MANNED BY SNIPERS AND INT. SEC. | |
| | | 1145 | REPRESENTATIVE FROM GREEN HOWARDS (50 DIV) VISITED BN. H.Q. | |
| | | | BN WARNED POSSIBILITY OF A MOVE IN NEAR FUTURE. | 6F/4 |
| | | 2000 | C.O. WENT TO BDE FOR ORDERS. | |
| | | 2115 | WARNING ORDER RECIEVED FOR BN TO CONCENTRATE IN AREA 728586 AND PREPARE TO PUSH FWD | |
| | | | ON A THRUST LINE TO ONDEFONTAINE 7849 | |
| 728586 | | 2330 | E.A. BOMBED VERY CLOSE TO BN. AREA. NO CASUALTIES. | |
| | 2 | 0115 | BN MOVED OFF AND PROCEEDED AT A STEADY PACE IN S.E. DIRECTION. | |
| | | 0600 | BN SCOUT CAR BLOWN UP AND ADJUTANT AND IC C.O. KILLED. | |
| | | 0915 | LEADING COY (A) ENCOUNTERED MINES AND M.G. NEAR JUQUES 7451. PATROLS PUSHED FWD | |
| | | | AND BN MOVED ON AT A SLOW PACE AGAINST STIFF OPPOSITION. | |
| 758505 | | 1700 | BN. H.Q. EST AT 758505 AND COYS FWD ON RIDGE | 7F/3 |
| | | 1915 | C.O. VISITED BDE. H.Q. | |
| | | | MAJ. TILLY (2 I/C) ASSUMED COMMAND OF THE BN. IN ABSENCE OF C.O. WHO RETURNED TO 'B' ECHELON | |
| | | | FOR A REST. | |
| | | 2230 | BN. STOOD TO UNTIL 0130 HRS. | |
| | 3 | 0410 | BN. STOOD TO UNTIL 0550 HRS. | |
| | | | SHELLING AND MORTARING THROUGHOUT MORNING. | |
| | | 1400 | BN. ATTACKED WITH THE INTENTION OF CLEARING WOODS TO SOUTH OF ONDEFONTAINE 7849 AND | |
| | | | ALSO TO OCCUPY VILLAGE. | |

The 4th Dorset's War Diary for the morning of 3 August simply states that at 0410 hrs the 'battalion stood to until 0550 hrs. Shelling and mortaring throughout morning'.

35th FDS (Field Dressing Station) there were now a total of eight surgeries working at the unit. A review at 0800 hrs on the 4th showed that 104 beds were occupied, of those cases about forty were abdominal cases requiring much attention. At about 1500 hrs, tents for two more wards arrived from No. 3 CCS.

By 2300 hrs on the 3rd, and still in No. 10 CCS, Bert's general condition had improved, despite being very badly wounded. 'To prepare for operation for surgeon to see' is the final remark on his medical report that day. The following morning he was transferred to the 25th FTU (Field Transfusion Unit), complaining of considerable pain, where he was given two blood transfusions at 0915 hrs (one pint) and 1400 hrs (three pints). In the afternoon of the 4th, and feeling more comfortable, Bert was transferred to 43rd Field Surgical Unit where he was operated on, the surgeon establishing for the first time the full extent of his injuries. Bert's wounds were redressed and the surgeon recommended post-operation physiotherapy, and sulphonamide therapy, to depress the activity of harmful bacteria. From the FTU he was evacuated by motor ambulance to the 79th British General Hospital, near Bayeux on 8 August, where on the 12th at 2030 hrs a second operation was carried out, as complications had set in with the partially aerated right lung, draining fluid away, and a sucking wound. All wounds were described as being rather unhealthy, with daily washouts administered to remove thick pus that was accumulating in the body. Despite being described as being 'very toxic and smelling', on 7 September it was decided that Bert should be evacuated by sea to England 'lying down', because of the nature of his injuries. Bert remained in the field hospital for a total of twenty-eight days, being tended by nurses of Queen Alexandra's Imperial Military Nursing Service (QAIMNS).

Royal Army Medical Corps nurses and women of the Queen Alexandra's Imperial Military Nursing Service (QAIMNS) carry a wounded soldier out of the operating tent at the 79th General Hospital at Bayeux, 20 June 1944. (Imperial War Museum B 5803)

The journey from the field hospital in Bayeux to the artificial harbour at Arromanches by motor ambulance, a distance of six miles, was particularly unpleasant as there was a chap in the bed underneath Bert's top bunk who smoked for the whole journey. This inconsiderate action by a fellow sufferer resulted in Bert coughing for the whole journey, as the cigarette smoke drifted upwards and into his damaged lung:

I was taken to a tent hospital near Bayeux where I was operated on for severe chest injuries. After staying there for several weeks I was shipped back to the United Kingdom and landed at Southampton. After spending one night in hospital there I went on a special hospital train to Edinburgh Royal Infirmary and eventually to a special chest unit at Bangour Hospital, which is between Glasgow and Edinburgh.

Wounded servicemen being transferred from motor ambulances to a hospital ship at the Mulberry artificial harbour at Arromanches, September 1944. (Imperial War Museum BU 1045)

In North-West Europe, 1944-45, RAMC (Royal Army Medical Corps) units were present at all levels, every infantry battalion had a Medical Officer (usually with the rank of Captain), a medical orderly, a 15cwt truck in which to carry their equipment, plus an NCO (Sergeant) and about twenty infantry men trained as stretcher bearers.

All soldiers were trained in simple first aid and the use of morphine, in addition to which they carried a First Field Dressing for immediate use, as well as a small bandage pack in a special pocket of the right leg of the battle dress trousers. In addition, a shell dressing, which was larger, was usually carried under the camouflage net that covered the steel helmet. Some vehicles also carried a boxed medical kit.

The wounded were collected by stretcher bearers and taken by Jeep or carrier to the Regimental Aid Post (RAP) where the Medical Officer (MO) and his orderly would give some immediate treatment. Depending on the severity of the wound, the

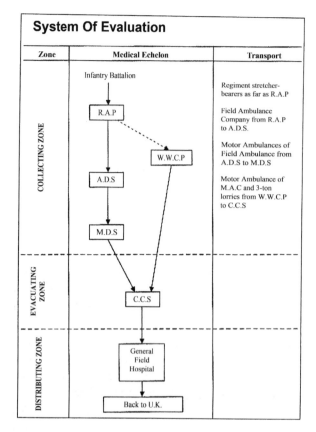

System of evaluation.

Field Ambulance personnel would evacuate the casualties to the Advanced Dressing Station (ADS) where they would then be collected by motor ambulance and taken to the Main Dressing Station (MDS). The headquarters of the Field Ambulance Company formed the Main Dressing Station (MDS), where casualties and their records were taken, anti-tetanus serum injected and urgent treatment given. After the treatment, the wounded were then transported to a Casualty Clearing Station (CCS). A Walking Wounded Collecting Post (WWCP) was usually set up about two to five miles from the frontline, to relieve pressure on the ADS during battle. Wounded were then collected by lorry and taken to the Casualty Clearing Station. From the CCS, casualties were then transported by Motor Ambulance Convoy (MAC), a Corps Unit, and taken to a General Field Hospital for further treatment or surgical operation. After treatment at the General Field Hospital the wounded were either moved to a Rest Station or a Convalescent Depot before returning to their unit. The more seriously wounded were evacuated back to UK by either ship or plane. The survival rate of the seriously wounded depended on how quickly professional medical treatment was received. In Normandy this was usually just one hour. Equally important were the three medical innovations of the time: penicillin and sulphanilamide (sulpha) to combat infection, and blood transfusion (plasma) to reduce shock.

# Chapter 8

# Return to Blighty

Bert was transferred from the 79th British General Hospital in France to the United Kingdom on the hospital carrier *St Julien*, disembarking at Southampton on 11 September. He was admitted to Royal South Hants and Southampton Hospital for an overnight stay before being transferred to the Thoracic (Chest) Unit, Cosham, Portsmouth, on the 12th. Bert had to be transferred by ship because his medical condition would not permit transfer by aeroplane. The *St Julien*, built in 1925 by Clydebank Engineering & Shipbuilders, was owned by the Great Western Railway Company, being used as a cross-channel ferry between Weymouth and the Channel Islands. It became a hospital carrier in 1939 and was returned to its owners in 1946, passing to British Railways on 1 January 1948. Hospital carriers were generally a passenger liner or merchant ship that had been fitted up as time and materials permitted. A hospital carrier was, in reality, an inferior type of hospital ship, which was a vessel specially designed and built, but more often a requisitioned liner, extensively adapted for the particular purpose of aiding sick and wounded. Hospital ships were in effect a floating hospital, medically and surgically equipped to deal with a wide range of cases of injury and disease.

The hospital ward in Southampton contained both British and German wounded soldiers, the Germans being segregated at one end. The Sister came on to the ward the morning after Bert's arrival and spoke to the patients, Bert responding with 'Good Morning Sister'. Her somewhat surprised response was to ask, 'What are you doing here?' as he'd been put in with the German wounded. Once he had been moved to the British section of the ward, Bert remembers several wounded Germans at the far end of the ward singing the song 'Silent Night' (*Stille Nacht*) in German. Mortar fragments had penetrated Bert's chest and damaged a lung, causing its collapse, which necessitated a tube being placed in the collapsed lung to wash it out every four hours. As a result Bert was unable to lie down in bed and had to remain sat upright, even during the night when he couldn't sleep because of the discomfort and pain and would pray for the morning to come to help alleviate his suffering. His chest was strapped with bandages to 'keep everything in place' and he remembers the agony when the Elastoplast was removed to change the bandages.

On 14 September Bert was transferred by hospital train to the Military Wing of the Royal Infirmary, Edinburgh (Thoracic Unit) and from there, on 26 September, to

Built in 1925 as a cross-channel ferry, the 1,885 ton *St Julien*, seen here quayside, was utilised as a hospital carrier during the war. (National Maritime Museum P23925)

Bangour Emergency Hospital, West Lothian (situated fourteen miles from Edinburgh in hilly woodlands near Broxburn). Located two miles west of Uphall and four miles east of Bathgate, Bangour Village Hospital was officially opened on 13 October 1906, as a Lunatic Asylum and in 1915 was taken over by the War Office as a military hospital. After the First World War, in commemoration of the vital role played by the hospital, Bangour Village Memorial Church was erected and opened in 1929. Bangour reopened as a psychiatric hospital in 1922. However, at the outbreak of war in September 1939 the hospital transformed, once again, into the Edinburgh War Hospital, with an additional emergency medical services annexe built on the hilltop site. The government feared that the casualties from the expected German Blitz would be so great that further emergency measures were deemed necessary and the Emergency Medical Service was quickly established to create thousands of extra beds in new temporary hospitals.

At the same time it was also decided to extend several existing hospitals, including Bangour Village Hospital, and so the Annexe, as it was first known, rapidly took shape on its hilltop site to the north-west of Bangour Home Farm in 1940. The 10th Annual Progress Report of the Edinburgh Public Health Committee, published in 1940, states, 'The Village Hospital has been adapted as a Base Hospital with 940 beds and the Department of Health are also erecting a hutted annexe in the vicinity of the farm.' The tenants of the farm cottages heard with some trepidation rumours of a hospital to be built in the Covert Field, concerned that they would lose the view of the Covert Wood with its kaleidoscope of colours as the seasons changed.

The five blocks of the Annexe, Bangour Village Hospital, in the distance, with Covert Wood beyond, taken in 1990.

Fortunately the long, low prefabricated buildings hid little of the woodland glory, but seemed to nestle into its shelter. As the war worsened the buildings were camouflaged and blended even more into the background. Five blocks, identified as 'P', 'Q', 'R', 'S' and 'T' blocks, each consisting of eight wards, were constructed at the Annexe. Sometime around the early spring of 1941 the first patients were admitted to Ward 1, 'Q' block of the Annexe. They were not Blitz victims or war casualties at all, but male surgical cases from West Lothian who were on the waiting list of the Edinburgh Royal Infirmary. From the summer of 1941 the other blocks began to fill, with the lower wards in 'S' block being taken over by the RAF, who staffed them with their own nursing sisters.

Dr Ian Thompson provides an interesting insight into an aspect of the hospital during wartime:

> The local units of the St Andrews Ambulance Association and Red Cross combined to form a single unit to provide first aid services as part of the Air Raid Precautions (ARP) units in the Uphall district. Dr Robert Thompson, my father, was lecturer to classes up to 150 strong. To keep the classes enthusiastic, training in home nursing was introduced. The men, mostly shale miners, formed a group of ambulance bearers, acquired a boiler suit uniform, and were on call to unload battle field patients from buses converted into ambulances. They would gather in Bangour Village Hospital early in the morning and await the arrival of buses from Waverley Station, Edinburgh. These wounded had been sent from the Dieppe or Normandy beaches, still in uniform, many with intravenous drips and in plaster of Paris

to immobilise their limb wounds in the Trueta style of battle first aid. The ambulance bearers had designed and rehearsed methods of stretcher bearing from bus to ward bed which was speedier and more efficient than standard drill. With the ward staff contacts made, these same men offered to assist in the ward nursing duties in their spare time. The civil nursing reserve was very short handed and welcomed the assistance in temperature recording, serving of meals, bed-making and even giving the troops bed baths. After the end of the hostilities these men acted as nursing auxiliaries unpaid, for nearly two years.

Bert spent his time as a patient at Bangour in 'Q' block and initially continued having washouts to take the fluids out of the lungs and Vaseline gauze applied every day to help heal the wounds on his back. Following an X-ray, on 19 September, a piece of shrapnel had been identified lying in the inferior (lower) part of Bert's chest. A further X-ray seven days later identified 'a metallic foreign body opposite ninth right rib in posterior axillary line' (the cavity beneath the junction of the arm and the body), which was removed in theatre on 29 November. Bert's medical history also records that part of the ninth rib was missing. In the emergency medical services, Annexe patients had to be wheeled from block to block for X-ray on a wire stretcher mounted on bicycle wheels – difficult to control especially when holding a drip. Two interesting healing aids, in addition to the wonderful nursing and medical care that Bert received, were artificial sunlight treatment which commenced on 29 October, and exercises for the unexpanded right lung from the Physiotherapy Department.

Bert recalls, 'I received wonderful treatment from everyone in Scotland as well as in France.' He particularly remembers the firm but very kind manner of Frances 'Frankie' Grant, Sister of the Annexe surgical ward in which he stayed during his prolonged recovery period. As Sister of Ward Q3, Sister Grant was renowned for her skills in resuscitation and wound care. Her nurses were always taught that there were three basics to nursing care and these were to ensure that patients were free of pain, could get adequate sleep and when awake were kept as comfortable as possible. There was also Sister Iona Gray, wife of surgeon Noel Gray, a theatre sister Bert remembers from his time spent at Bangour. She recalled in particular the terrible shortages with which the staff had to work. 'Even the swabs were washed, sterilised and used again. Hours and hours were taken up washing bandages and then carefully ironing them ready to be used again'.

Local families were asked to visit the wounded servicemen in hospital and on one of his regular visits to the hospitalised Methodists, the Methodist minister from nearby Armadale, the Revd Arthur Valle (who was afterwards transferred to Redfield Methodist Church, Bristol, and helped officiate at Bert and Joyce's wedding) explained to Bert that he knew a lady who worked in 'The Shop' down at the main hospital and that he was going to ask her to come and visit.

Bert didn't normally get any visitors as he was so far from his home and family in Bristol, although his sister Alice and brother Cliff once visited him in hospital, staying overnight in Scotland before returning to Bristol the next day.

'I remember three ladies coming into the ward dressed in fur coats bearing all sorts of gifts. This was a wonderful family, that were so kind to me and when I was better they invited me into their house.' 'Milly' Henderson, and her two married daughters Lena Baynham and Isabel Fleming, who all lived in nearby Bathgate, were

The Revd Arthur Valle, taken in 1941, two years before he became Methodist minister at Armadale, West Lothian.

the three ladies who visited Bert that day and continued to do so throughout his stay in Scotland. Amelia 'Milly' and her husband David 'Davie' Henderson, who lived in Fettes Cottage, Mill Lane, in the north-west edge of Bathgate, had three children, Lena, married to Bill Baynham, Isabel – known as 'Bunty' – married to Charles 'Chick' Fleming, and their only son, Marshall. It was 'Bunty' who worked in the shop at the entrance to the hospital.

It was only after Bert was permitted to go visiting the Henderson family that he met Marshall and his fiancée, Nan. They struck up a firm friendship, so much so that Bert was asked by Marshall to be his best man when he got married. Another local individual who befriended Bert and demonstrated great kindness and thoughtfulness towards him during his prolonged stay in Scotland was Jenny, who worked in Bangour Hospital as a cleaner. Jenny also lived in Bathgate, with her mother, and it was only after her mother's death that she married her long-standing fiancé, Jimmy Wilson.

'Aunt' Milly used to visit a local homeopathic doctor and on a couple of occasions was accompanied by Bert, when the doctor gave him some homeopathic medicine to help alleviate the breathing problems he was experiencing due to the injuries sustained to his chest. When the doctor learnt that Bert was a Bristolian he remarked to 'Milly' that Bristol 'was a lovely city but the worst place for breathing'.

When Bert was able to get up and about after being bed-ridden for seven and a half months he was transferred to Wallhouse, a large private house a mile to the west of Torphichen village and three miles north of Bathgate, to convalesce. When discharged from hospital, he recalls having to make the ten-mile trip from Bangour Hospital to Wallhouse, via Bathgate, by public transport, and having great difficulty pronouncing the name of his destination, had to show the address to the bus driver. Wallhouse (originally Well-house), was a ten-bedroom castellated mansion, with battlements festooned with gargoyles, a lofty square tower, and walled garden. Built in the 1840s and set in acres of parkland, the house contained heraldic coats of arms, ornate plasterwork and beautiful stained glass windows. The house was full of recovering patients and Bert shared a bedroom with four other convalescents,

'The Shop', where 'Bunty' Fleming worked, was located at the main entrance to Bangour Village Hospital.

The Henderson family of Bathgate taken in the 1960s. From left to right, back row: Charles 'Chick' Fleming, Nan Henderson, Bill Baynham, Marshall Henderson. Front row: Isabel 'Bunty' Fleming, Davie Henderson, Amelia 'Milly' Henderson, Lena Baynham. David and Stuart Henderson, sons of Marshall and Nan, are the two boys.

remarking that the food was very good there. However, life at Wallhouse wasn't only rest and recuperation, as Bert was given chores to do in the house, such as cleaning the brass, no doubt as an aid to his rehabilitation.

On transferring to Wallhouse he was allowed to go out for the first time. 'Bunty' Fleming who was friendly with the matron, Mrs Stewart, would ring her up and ask if they could have Mr Haddrell out for the day. On his outings to Bathgate, Bert would be dressed in his 'hospital blues' – blue uniform, white shirt and red tie.

Other trips included invitations to the Usher Hall in Edinburgh on Sunday evenings to see variety concerts and on one occasion Isabel Bailey, the soprano opera star, singing 'the Messiah'. The patients were transported to and from Edinburgh and when they walked down into the hall the spotlight was put on them, as they were wearing their 'hospital blues'. On another occasion, the girls at P.T.'s (Patrick Thompsons), a large store in Edinburgh, invited the soldiers for a meal at their restaurant and then took them to see a show at a theatre afterwards.

Socially, the mobile wounded were entertained in the surrounding towns and villages by concerts, dances and whist drives. A minor problem was the reaction of local citizens, unused to meeting severely handicapped or disfigured patients. A weekly dance was held in the Recreation Hall in Bangour Village Hospital. During the evening a consultant surgeon would pop his head in the door, study the dancers and on Monday morning certain patients would be listed RTU (Return to Unit), having lost their limps in a quickstep.

Whilst convalescing at Torphichen, two ribs that had been operated on in France were causing Bert some discomfort so the surgeon, Mr Noel Gray, sent for him to return to hospital where he operated, chiselling out the jagged piece of the ribs.

Wallhouse, Torphichen, a large private house built in the 1840s, used as a convalescent home during the war.

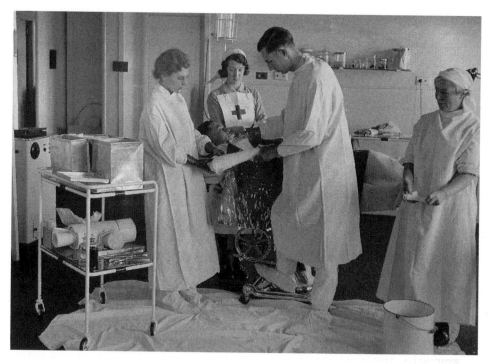

Staff at Bangour Village Hospital, including surgeon Mr Noel Gray, putting a plaster cast on a patient's arm, *c.* 1949. Jean C. Millar is on the left.

Noel Gray, one of the hospital's most affectionately remembered surgeons, arrived at Bangour in June 1940, acting as senior to two other Registrars, all three having been invited to join the Emergency Medical Service's staff by the Surgical Director, Sir Henry Wade. He arrived at Bangour from Nottingham General Hospital and during the summer and autumn of 1940 was occupied with treating the remainder of the Dunkirk gunshot wounds. As Bangour was officially a military hospital, Mr Gray recalled in 1991 what he described as, 'the rather anomalous position of having one's work inspected by senior Army and Navy officers, who were concerned that civilians were being allowed to treat service personnel with serious injuries.' Noel Gray, a member of the original Annexe staff, who subsequently devoted the whole of his distinguished career to Bangour General Hospital, retired in October 1976.

On 7 May 1945 Germany surrendered and 8 May was declared VE Day (Victory in Europe). On that date, massive celebrations took place, notably in London, where over a million people celebrated in a carnival atmosphere the end of the European war, though rationing of food and clothing was to continue for a number of years. In London crowds massed, in particular in Trafalgar Square and up the Mall to Buckingham Palace, where King George VI and Queen Elizabeth, accompanied by the Prime Minister, Winston Churchill, appeared on the balcony of the palace to cheering crowds. Princess Elizabeth (the future Queen Elizabeth II) and her sister, Princess Margaret, were allowed to wander anonymously among the crowds and take part in the celebrations in London.

Bert whilst convalescing in Scotland wearing his Army great coat over his hospital 'blues' – light blue uniform, white shirt and red tie.

Bert's experience of VE Day was somewhat different:

My memory of VE Day is rather sad: like everyone else I was glad that the war had ended but it was a rather sad occasion for me. I was in a convalescent home in Torphichen, near Bathgate, West Lothian. I had been in hospital for a year (seven and a half months confined to bed) after being wounded in the invasion of France, but was making progress.

Whilst in hospital I made friends with another young fellow who came from Dunfermline (also named Bert) and as I came from Bristol I did not have many visitors. When his mother visited him, she would talk to me as well and invariably brought me some fruit, sweets, etc., which I greatly appreciated, being so far from home. When her son, Bert, went home for a weekend I was invited as well and she was very kind to me, making me most welcome as only Scots people can.

I met her other son, who was in the Army, and stationed somewhere in England. Soon after this he was on Army exercises, and was tragically drowned. I had only known him slightly but I think that, perhaps because I had been in the Forces, they asked me if I would attend his funeral. I felt it was the right and proper thing to do out of courtesy, and the funeral was fixed for what turned out to be VE Day.

I had to make my own way from Bathgate to Dunfermline (a distance of approximately twenty-five miles) by public transport, which was a restricted service, and took quite a long time. However, I did get there in time for the funeral and paid my respects. The family treated me very well, even in the midst of their grief, were most particular to look after me, and were very grateful for the fact that I had attended the funeral. After the service I had to make the return journey by public transport, and arrived back quite late at the convalescent home at Torphichen.

My VE Day memory was tinged with sadness, but it is a day I will never forget. The war in Europe was over, I had survived, though wounded, whereas many of my comrades had paid the supreme sacrifice, and looked forward to going home. I was just twenty years old, and was discharged as unfit for military service on the 26 July 1945.

Bert left Scotland, resplendent in his newly acquired 'demob' suit, shirt, tie and shoes, having spent a year in Scotland hospitalized and convalescing, travelling back to his home in Bristol by railway from Waverley Station, Edinburgh – and had to stand or sit on his suitcase for the whole journey as nobody had reserved a seat for him and there were no available seats. He found the whole experience 'very trying'.

Bert's return from the war was a touch on the genteel side. The fond image of the ex-serviceman walking back up the garden path in his 'demob' suit to an enthusiastic welcome from the family he left behind didn't always happen. Bert's two unmarried brothers, Cliff and Arthur, were still serving in the Armed Forces, his father was out, and so he arrived home to find only his mother waiting to greet him, although welcome enough as he hadn't seen her for over a year. The reunion was short-lived however, as Alice – as she was now known – died in October the same year.

Bert was discharged from the Army on 26 July 1945 as 'ceasing to fulfil Army physical requirements' with a 100% War Pension. The report by the Invaliding Medical Board following his examination was, 'Assessment - 100% for Gunshot [sic] Wounds Chest, attributable to War Service'. This percentage was reduced, and as a result his

Edinburgh Castle, Princes Street, on the right, and Waverley Railway Station, bottom left, 1947.

pension was also, as his health improved over the years, but later it was increased again because of Bilateral Sensori Neural hearing loss attributed to the effects of artillery fire whilst serving in the Army.

His service with the colours was from 6 May 1943 to 26 July 1945 (totalling two years and eighty-two days), and for his service in the North-West Europe theatre, between 19 June and 10 September 1944, he was awarded the 1939/45 Star, the France and Germany Star, the 1939/45 War Medal, and the Defence Medal (for service in World War II). His discharge certificate, issued by the Infantry Record Office, Exeter on 4 June 1945, describes his military conduct as 'Very Good'. Along with his campaign medals, Bert received a letter from the Minister of Pensions stating that he had been commanded by His Majesty the King to forward him the King's Badge, a round silver lapel badge with the Royal cipher surmounted with the words, 'For Loyal Service', which was issued to members of the Armed Forces who were disabled as a result of war service undertaken since 3 September 1939. He wears this badge with pride.

Bert recommenced employment with H.J. Packer & Company in September 1945, working in the overdue accounts section of the firm. The outbreak of the Second World War in September 1939 was followed by the introduction of the Control of Raw Materials, which affected production of both Packer's and Bond's lines. Charles Bond Ltd was a subsidiary company set up to manufacture and supply high class chocolate products. Consequently, with certain items in short supply, the decision was taken to withdraw the Packer's grade from the market, and only Bond's goods were manufactured from 1939. As chocolate was a rationed commodity the firm introduced its own scheme in order to ensure absolutely fair and proportionate distribution to every customer, and this was more than justified by the many expres-

Bert Haddrell as a post-war civilian wearing the King's Badge in his coat lapel.

The King's Badge – issued to
members of the Armed Forces
who were disabled as a result
of war service.

sions of appreciation subsequently received by the company. Many male factory
workers were called to fight, leaving production in mainly female hands. Rationing
did stabilise demand, and sales were boosted by orders from the Army. Nevertheless,
overall output did diminish, and later in the war part of the Greenbank factory was
taken over by the American Army, before hostilities finally ceased in 1945.

The immediate post-war years of austerity proved very difficult for Packer's, along
with the whole of the confectionery industry. The industry stagnated until the
removal of controls on raw materials and the lifting of rationing on confectionary
products at the beginning of 1953. Consequently, the whole period was dominated
by the continual struggle to remain viable, with very little money available to invest
in a new plant and equipment at Greenbank. The factory's 1,100 or so employees
(830 of which were women) were struggling to cope with outdated production
methods. Nevertheless, although since the start of the war only Bond's lines had been
produced, with the removal of the last vestiges of food rationing in July 1954 it was
felt by the latter part of 1955 that the time was right to reintroduce the Packer's grade,
for which it was believed a large demand existed.

Bert recalls that Packers were very understanding and helpful on his return to the
company following his Army service, allowing him to work part-time with no loss
of wages. His medical report of August 1946 records that 'Bert has a day or two off
every couple of weeks because of pain and difficulty with breathing in close weather.'
A year later, in October 1947, Bert still hadn't returned to full-time work and in
consideration of his indifferent health and tendency to absence was engaged on light
clerical duties, five days per week, 9.00 a.m to 3.30 p.m., instead of 5.30 p.m., with
an hour for lunch. The clinical finding of the Ministry Medical Board that month
was that the expansion of his right lower lung was still very poor, and even though

his overall health was reasonable they found that 'the effect of pensionable disability on function was "considerable"'. As a consequence he was assessed as 60 per cent disabled. Following this assessment, Bert appealed under the Pensions Tribunal Act, as in view of his condition the present assessment was inadequate as it did not express the full degree of disablement. But following a review in March 1948 the disability assessment was maintained at 60 per cent. A further appeal lodged later that year also proved unsuccessful.

On 27 March 1946 Bert reached the age of twenty-one, receiving from his father the princely sum of 2s 6d as his birthday present. Bert met his future wife, Joyce that same year at the University Settlement club in Barton Hill, Bristol. The club, run by two university students, was primarily for returning ex-service personnel and as well as a weekly club night, provided activities such as a drama group, rambles, outings, and tennis. Both Bert and Joyce saw an advertisement for the club in the Bristol Evening Post newspaper. Joyce attended the club with her cousin, Olive Begley, and friend Hilda Emery, and she and Bert had known each other for a while before he asked her out:

> We went to the BBC recording studios in Whiteladies Road, Clifton for an evening visit with the club. On the way back to the club from the BBC we stopped on the Centre and I plucked up the courage to ask her to go to the pictures. She said yes, I am pleased to say, and we went out for the first time on the Friday night. It was a date that led to marriage two years later, but neither of us can remember what the film was that we saw. It was at His Majesty's cinema in Stapleton Road, Eastville.

Joyce Hale was born in Bristol on 18 November 1926, the daughter of Ernest and Annie Hale (née Young). Her parents owned their own modest home, No. 9 Parsons Street, off Stapleton Road, having purchased it for £99 with an interest free loan from Ernest's father, Albert Charles Hale. On finishing her secondary education at Newfoundland Road Girls School, Joyce won £20 towards a year's training at Cannings' College, a commerce college at the top of Park Street. Fees for the year were approximately £26 and Joyce received a letter offering her a place, commencing in September 1940. Pupils wore a uniform of blazer and tie, with a felt hat in winter and Panama hat in summer, both adorned with a blue and gold hat band. The college taught girls commercial and secretarial skills such as book-keeping, 'Greggs' shorthand, and touch typing. One of the techniques employed by the teachers was to cover the typewriter keyboard, requiring students to type to music which, as training advanced, became progressively quicker. One important aspect of the course was the regular spelling homework that all students were required to undertake. Joyce used to walk to the college in Park Street with two other girls, one of whom, Audrey Wollacott, lived close by.

The first major air-raid on Bristol took place on Sunday 24 November 1940. That evening Joyce and her friend Audrey Fricker informed their parents that they would be attending the service at their local church, St Clements in Newfoundland Road. However, their intention was to spend the hour and a half not at church, but elsewhere having a bit of fun, but at about 6 p.m., as Joyce got to Audrey's house in St Lawrence Street, St Pauls, the same road in which Joyce's cousins the Begleys lived, the German bombing raid started. Joyce, together with Audrey, Audrey's parents and her brother, went straight to the Frickers air-raid shelter where they spent most of the night in safety. Joyce was wearing a new green coat and, unbeknown to her, Mr Fricker had that day painted the inside of the shelter with light green paint, which she duly got on her coat. The bombing eased off around 4 a.m., when Joyce took the opportunity to run home, greatly concerned as to what her mother would say about getting wet paint on her new coat, imagining she would 'play hell' with her. Annie, of course, was so pleased that her daughter had arrived home safely that she was not at all concerned about the paint, just greatly relieved after ten hours of agonizing and uncertainty. Hugging Joyce she said, 'It doesn't matter about your coat, as long as you're safe'.

When Joyce made her way through the destruction on the Monday morning to attend college, she found that the college building had been destroyed during the night-time bombing raid. All students were subsequently offered a place, to continue the course at one of two alternative Cannings' Colleges located in Bath and Chippenham. Joyce chose to attend the college at Northumberland Buildings, Queen Square, travelling by bus to Bath. The daily journey involved walking from her home in Parsons Street to Lawrence Hill to catch the bus, a journey of about fifteen miles at a cost of 5*d* (half-fare) one way; a tiring routine particularly following a day's tuition.

As the frequency of air-raids increased, Joyce's mother wanted to make arrangements for her daughter to stay with Annie's brother, Percy Young, and his wife Rose, who lived in Bath, so that Joyce could continue attending college. However, Joyce wasn't that keen on the idea of living with her aunt and uncle, and Bath was also suffering from the Blitz, so alternative arrangements were made. Joyce had made friends with a girl who also attended Cannings' College, Beryl Luker, who lived in Upton Cheyney, a small village between Bristol and Bath, approximately six miles from the college. Beryl said, 'Why don't you come and live with us?', which meant that Joyce didn't have such a long journey to college and was protected from the ever-increasing German bombing raids. The Luker family lived in a house in the village, with Mrs Luker's mother and her brother Charlie living next door. Beryl had an older brother, Alan, and a younger sister, Myra, and the whole Luker family attended chapel every Sunday. The Lukers ran a general store from a converted downstairs room, selling groceries and a multitude of other items. Joyce recalls the lovely garden of the house and the happy time she spent there. It was a very different environment from the terraced house in central Bristol which was Joyce's home.

During Joyce's stay at Upton Cheyney her mother brought news that the church they attended in Bristol, St Clements', had been totally destroyed. Because of its proximity to the city centre, the St Paul's area suffered badly during the air-raids of the Second World War, particularly during the bombardment of 11/12th April 1941 (known locally as the 'Good Friday Raid') when Newfoundland Road and Houlton Street bore the brunt of the attack and St Clements' Church was destroyed. The church had played a significant part in the lives of the Hale family; it was where they worshipped on a Sunday, Joyce's brother Stanley played the organ there, and Joyce attended Sunday school, Brownies, Girl Guides and took part in activities such as plays and concerts. Joyce's mother was also very involved with the church, sewing and crocheting items to sell at the annual 'Sale of Work' to raise funds for the church. The destruction of St Clements' was a devastating blow as family, relatives and friends all went to the church in Newfoundland Road.

As the situation in Bristol became even more dangerous, Joyce's parents, Ernest and Annie, travelled to Upton Cheney to stay overnight in order to avoid the night time bombing raids, and were put up in the Lukers' front room. They would then get up very early in the morning, and walk down to the main Bath Road to catch the bus back to Bristol. Annie would return to the family home, whilst Ernest went to work as a wood machinist. As the threat of German bombs receded Ernest and Annie's overnight stays became less frequent.

As her time at Cannings' College was drawing to a close, Joyce's mother had to find an additional £6 for her to finish the course and receive her certificates. Joyce successfully passed all of her examinations and was given a testimonial on 21 July 1941 by the Headmaster, P.G. (Philip George) Maggs. He recorded that she was able to write shorthand at the rate of 100 words a minute, use a typewriter quickly and accurately, and had a good knowledge of the principles of double entry book-keeping and general office routine. Summing up, he wrote that he had every confidence in putting her name forward to prospective employers as a junior shorthand-typist. Returning to Bristol with her new qualifications and glowing testimonial, Joyce soon found employment, commencing work at Legal & General Assurance Society Ltd in Baldwin Street, typing and taking shorthand for a Miss Tye with wages of £1 per week, rising to £1 5s after six weeks. After a while the company moved to Clevedon in North Somerset, where they had bought a big house, moving all their records there for safety as the bombing still continued. Joyce now had to catch the train to work at 9 a.m. from Temple Meads station to Weston-super-Mare, changing at Yatton to get the local train to Clevedon, returning to Bristol at about 5.30 p.m. in the evening. On one occasion, whilst chatting in the waiting room at Temple Meads, they all missed the train to work and had to catch the next one.

When the weather was fine Joyce and other girls from the office would walk the short distance to the seafront where they would sit and eat their sandwiches. As staff got increasingly fed up with the travelling from Bristol and found other jobs, local people were employed by the company, many of whom where not particularly enamoured with the idea of working at all. One such lady, the daughter of a Tickenham pub landlord, used to come to work 'all dressed up wearing jewels' with no idea of what office work entailed and not really wanting to be there. During the war, if a woman was single or married with no children she was required to work to help with the war effort, the influx of women into the workplace freeing men to be called up. Joyce was the only one of her immediate family who worked in an office, as her female cousins in the Bragg and Begley families worked in factories such as W.D. & H.O. Wills Tobacco Factory in Bedminster, where the yearly bonus was greatly prized, even though the hours were long and hard. Joyce eventually got fed up with travelling to Clevedon every day and as commercial and secretarial jobs were plentiful at the time, found employment at Atlas Assurance Co. Ltd in Clare Street, just off the centre in Bristol.

In 1943 Joyce, together with a friend and her cousin, joined a local Women's Junior Air Corps (WJAC) unit based at Eastville Junior Mixed School, Coombe Road. The WJAC was a uniformed youth organisation aimed at girls of secondary school age and upwards, teaching elementary drill, Morse Code and aircraft recognition from cards with silhouettes on them. The uniform consisted of black shoes, grey skirt, blue shirt, tie and grey forage cap. Joyce recalls spending most of her time whilst with the unit marching and parading, although there were also various social events.

Joyce's elder brother, Stanley Hale, was employed by Harry Willis as a painter and decorator, a job designated as being a reserved occupation. A reserved occupation was an occupation considered important enough to the country that those employed in it were exempt from military service. In the UK, in 1938, a *Schedule of Reserved Occupations* had been drawn up, exempting certain key skilled workers from conscription.

Joyce and Bert became engaged to be married in January 1948, from that date spending all of their time together, except for Monday evenings when Bert attended the University Settlement drama group, something that Joyce was not particularly interested in. Despite being twenty-one years old, Joyce still had to be home by 10 p.m., even when engaged. For her twenty-first birthday Joyce's parents organised a party,

Joyce Hale, aged nineteen years, taken at Weston-super-Mare, 15 July 1946.

saving precious ration coupons for the cake and food. Unfortunately, her father was laid off work that very day, but didn't say anything to anyone, so as not to spoil the excitement of the occasion. There was even a barrel of beer which was rolled from their home to the church hall. During their courtship, Bert wooed Joyce with chocolate from Packer's, being a particularly tasty treat as chocolate was rationed at the time. He was able to obtain what were called 'mis-shapes' or 'seconds', chocolate that couldn't be sold, with the added bonus that Bert didn't have to use up ration points for the chocolate that he was able to buy from the factory. A particular favourite were Walnut Whips without the walnuts! Bert would also send to Valetta, the capital of Malta, for stockings for Joyce as buying them abroad didn't require using one's ration coupons.

Marshall Henderson in Scotland asked Bert to be best man at his wedding on 18 September 1948 at Armadale, near Bathgate, and Bert and Joyce decided to plan a holiday to Scotland to coincide with the wedding, as Joyce hadn't met the Scots folks who had been so kind to her future husband. They then decided to get married themselves, the week before Nan and Marshall, and make the trip to Scotland their honeymoon. To have a new suit made for his wedding Bert needed to use some of his allocation of clothes coupons, as well as being able to find a tailor with cloth to make a suit. Bill Baynham in Bathgate knew of somebody who could make a suit for

The wedding of Bert Haddrell and Joyce Hale, 11 September 1948, St Agnes Church, Bristol. From left to right, back row: Irene Haddrell (née Wilkey), Arthur Haddrell, Arthur Heales, Stanley Hale. Front row: Frederick Haddrell, Alice Heales (née Haddrell), Bert Haddrell, Joyce Hale, Peggy Hale (née Masters), Clifford Haddrell, Annie Hale, Ernest Hale. The girl in front is Sandra Hale.

Bert Haddrell, outside Fettes Cottage, Mill Lane, Bathgate, the home of Davie and 'Milly' Henderson, whilst on holiday in Scotland, June 1946, wearing a black watch tartan kilt.

Bert, so he sent his measurements and coupons to Scotland where his wedding suit was duly made.

Herbert Henry Haddrell married Joyce Lilian Annie Hale on 11 September 1948 at St Agnes Church, St Pauls, Bristol, and amongst those attending the wedding was the Revd Arthur Valle who had befriended Bert when in hospital in Scotland. Joyce's wedding dress was hired, so that clothing coupons could be used to buy a brown two-piece suit which she wore to go on honeymoon. The wedding reception was in the church hall, a colleague of Bert's at Packers making the wedding cake, a luxury not enjoyed by many newlywed couples, it being a time of austerity and of making-do, with cardboard wedding cakes in vogue. Bert remembered how those close to him rallied around to help provide sufficient provisions, 'Food was still in very short supply, so friends and relatives helped out'.

The first time that Joyce met the Henderson 'clan' at Fettes Cottage in Bathgate, everybody sat down to a meal and were talking so excitedly that she couldn't under-

The Haddrell
brothers at a family
wedding in 1965.
From left to right:
Clifford, Frederick,
Thomas, Arthur
and Bert.

stand a word that was being said due to the combination of their Scots accent and
speaking so quickly. A party piece Bert and Joyce entertained the family with that
evening was a rendition of 'Fire, Fire' played as a duet on the piano.

Bert and Joyce began their married life with Joyce's parents (Ernest and Annie
Hale) at 9 Parsons Street, near Stapleton Road, before buying their first home at
No. 53 York Road, Easton, where they were living when both their children were
born. Bert and Joyce celebrated their sixtieth wedding anniversary in September
2008; they have a son, Ian, a daughter Claire, two granddaughters, Georgina and Sally,
and a grandson, Benjamin.

# Chapter 9

# Remembrance

In spite of receiving frightful life-threatening injuries in Normandy, Bert considers himself to be one of the lucky ones of the generation that were called to war between 1939 and 1945, as despite his disablement he has been able to lead a long and fulfilled life. Lucky in so much that he survived the war when so many of his contemporaries did not, and countless individuals suffered afterwards throughout their lives. Remembrance for him is deeply personal, recalling fallen comrades and the brother he lost, and the price they paid for freedom.

Bert has been Secretary of the Staple Hill branch of the Royal British Legion for over twenty years and is Secretary of the Bristol Branch No. 2 of the Normandy Veterans Association. He thoroughly enjoys the unique comradeship and camaraderie of the men who fought in Normandy and has made a good many friends in both organisations. He is also a member of 43rd Wessex Association.

As well as continuing to collect for the annual Royal British Legion's Poppy Appeal, he visits local schools to talk to the children about his wartime experiences, the importance of remembrance and to make future generations aware of the horrors of war. The oral tradition that connects us to these events fades by degrees and the duty of remembrance devolves to those of us who thankfully have not known war:

It was all sixty-five years ago and sometimes I wonder whether it was all real; it feels so far removed. I was just an ordinary person, doing the duty that I had to do.

We don't think we were heroes. We just had a job to do and we tried to do it well.

It is important to go because 2009 will probably be one of the last times so many veterans of the conflict will be able to attend the Second World War remembrance ceremonies.

I know there will be a mixture of pride and emotion when we're in Normandy. It will be the chance to remember all those people who made the sacrifice of their lives.

The badge of
the Dorsetshire
Regiment.

The badge of
the Normandy
Veterans
Association.

When I came to I was badly wounded but I didn't know this, and all my comrades were killed. I said a little prayer, which sounds funny now, I said, 'Please God I'm not afraid to die but don't let me die in a foreign country'. Strangely enough since I've been back I wouldn't have minded because the graves are kept so beautifully.

Bert Haddrell at the grave of Roy Bartlett, St Manvieu War Cemetery, Cheux, Normandy, July 1994.

Private 5735215 Roy Bartlett, the son of Frederick John and Ellen Elizabeth Bartlett, of Colway Mead, Dorsetshire, was killed in action on 10 July 1944, aged twenty-one years.

Bert Haddrell and fellow Normandy veterans being presented with commemorative medals at l'Abbaye aux Dames, Caen, July 1994. Created by Le Conseil Régional de Basse-Normandie (Regional Council of Lower Normandy) to honour veterans of the invasion of Normandy, on the front of the medal are inscribed 'Overlord 6 Juin 1944' and the names of the landing beaches. On the reverse side is the Torch of Freedom surrounded by the device of William the Conqueror, 'Diex Aie' ('God is with us' in Norman French).

Normandy veterans Bert Haddrell and Henry Pring promoting the 'Heroes Return' scheme, 9 February 2004. The Lottery-funded scheme helped to pay for Second World War veterans to visit the battlefields where they served.

Veterans of the 4th and 5th Battalions, Dorsetshire Regiment on the summit of Hill 112, 11 July 2004, commemorate the sixtieth anniversary of the battle for the infamous hill. Bert Haddrell is third from the left.

HRH Prince Edward, the Earl of Wessex, talking to Bert Haddrell on Hill 112, 11 July 2004.

Kenneth Hay, Frank Porter and
Bert Haddrell – veterans of the 4th
Dorsets – stand behind the graves
of fallen comrades of the Dorset
Regiment, St Manvieu War Cemetery,
July 2004.

Bert Haddrell receiving his
commemorative chest badge from
a French official of the Normandie
Mémoire 60ème Anniversaire
organization at the commemoration
ceremony on Hill 112, 11 July 2004.

43rd Wessex Monument. This monument is dedicated to the soldiers of the 43rd Wessex Division, who gave their lives for freedom in June and July 1944, in the fighting for the capture of Château de Fontaine, and the liberation of Maltot and Éterville. It is located on the summit of Hill 112 near the D8 road, in Baron-sur-Odon area.

Detail of the 43rd Wessex Monument showing the carved Wyvern.

The inscription on the 43rd Wessex Monument. The 43rd Division had the highest number of fatal casualties of all divisions in the British 2nd Army in Normandy – at least 1,727. The division also lost the highest number of Battalion Commanders in Normandy – eight killed in action or died of wounds, four of them during Operation Jupiter.

A plaque in Cheux town centre near the town hall recalls the action of the 43rd Wessex Division on 27 June 1944 (the 5th Battalion the Duke of Cornwall's Light Infantry and the 1st Battalion the Worcestershire Regiment).

Plaque au Dorset Regiment, Éterville. This plaque is in memory of the soldiers of the Dorset Regiment who fought for the liberation of Éterville in July 1944. It is located in the centre of the village on the town hall wall.

## When You Go Home

The following poem was composed in 2004, by Kenneth Hay MBE JP, to commemorate the sixtieth anniversary of the Normandy campaign. Ken Hay served as a Private with the 2/4th Essex Regiment from May 1943 to April 1944, with the 4th Dorsets from April 1944 to August 1945, and as a Corporal with the Royal Corps of Signals from August 1945 to July 1947. He was interned in Kgf Stalag VIII B Teschen, Poland from July 1944 to May 1945.

> We that were left grow old – but, then, we've mostly lived our lives
> With sons and daughters, grand-kids too, all stemming from our wives.
> We've built careers and bought a house and holidayed many places,
> We've bought our televisions, cars as well; whilst some kicked over traces.
>
> When not at work, we've watched the team or practised DIY,
> Painted the house, constructed things, whatever caught our eye.

Tilly-sur-Seulles War Cemetery. There was heavy and fluctuating fighting in the vicinity of Tilly-sur-Seulles immediately after the D-Day landings, chiefly involving the 49th and 50th Divisions. The cemetery contains 990 Commonwealth burials (including twenty-three 4th Dorsets) of the Second World War and 232 German graves.

We've served as councillors, sat on the bench or worked in charities
Or other interests we acquired to occupy our ease.

But, not forgetting comradeship, we joined ex-service bodies
To keep alive the joys we knew when we were merely squaddies,
We've brought our pints and had our laughs, and fought old battles often
But, through, the years, we've kept in mind those not to be forgotten.

To Normandy we've gone oft times – that path we took before
To meet again those welcoming French whose thanks last evermore,
It's good to shake their hands once more and share in their bonheur,
To sit and sup, to sing our songs and drink their vin d'honneur.

But never do we question why we journey 'cross the waves
'tis why you'll find us stood in tears, head bowed, among the graves,
And as we look at those sad stones, we ask the question why
Why me that stands above in life – whilst they in death do lie?

Sadly they lie in foreign fields, beneath a foreign soil
Their stones record the names and dates they parted from life's toil.
They gave their all, that you and I would live a life of peace
But what a sacrifice to make – when such young lives just cease.

This one's a number close to mine and I was his age, eighteen years,
Others with wife and family whose death caused bitter tears.
That one wore the badge I wore, which still I wear with pride,
Whilst there they are, their badge in stone, a-standing side by side.

Most of them just never knew the thrill of female charms
They never cradled baby son, or girl, in loving arms,
They never felt a rounded breast or shared a rapturous kiss,
Some never loved at all – what happiness they missed!

They went to their graves, no family there, for they were far away
Buried with care but stranger-borne, no tears shed on that day,
The tears came later – when Mums and Dads received the tragic news
And many a parent broke their heart, a cherished son to lose.

Whene'er I drove through Dorsetshire, or England's friendly dales
I think of lads who left these farms and folk, put final hay in bales,
Kissed Mum good-bye, perhaps a girl, gave Dad a hug, and off to war
They did not know, they never feared, they'd tramp those fields no more.

This is the England that they loved, for which they gave their lives,
Entrusting Governments to tend their kids and compensate their wives.
But time and time these trusting souls have had their trust betrayed,
If they returned to our sad world, they'd surely be dismayed.

I have no doubt that they would see their deaths an awful waste,
'For this we died', 'You do not joke', 'It leaves a nasty taste',
'We gave the lot, lives, wives and kids, and years of happiness,
Why have those that followed on created such a mess?'

'So here we lie, stilled for all time, under this foreign sod,
Some with number, name above – some known but to God.
Keep us in mind whene'er you pray – as we will pray for thee
That, at the last trump, we'll meet again here in eternity'.

When you go home, tell them of us and say
For you your tomorrow, we gave our today.

# The Hat

This poem was written by Joyce Haddrell in 2005 to commemorate the sixtieth anniversary of both VE Day and VJ Day.

I had a phone call a few weeks ago,
From the 43rd Wessex Association,
Inviting me, with a guest, to the 60th Anniversary celebrations
Of the end of the Second World War.

It was to be held at Horse Guards Parade in London,
At 3 o'clock on Sunday the 10th July,
Morning dress or lounge suits with medals to be worn by men,
And day dresses with hats by the ladies.

As time went by our official tickets arrived,
And we remembered what we were expected to wear,
A lounge suit and day dress now that would be fine,
But a hat, that was different, something my wife never wears.

We had a look around and eventually found
The right colour blue, size and shape to match her dress,
And so we were ready for our special event,
Lift arranged, coach seats booked, passports ready for identification.

Veterans of the Forces and Home Front, who were young in the forties,
Came from all walks of life on that day,
To reflect and remember and shed silent tears,
For friends and comrades who never would return.

The ladies were glad of their hats, with temperatures up in the thirties,
There were few empty seats and a sense of defiance,
As we remembered the shocking events of the 7th July,
And prayed for the victims and their families.

We listened to the Declaration of War in 1939,
To Churchill's stirring message after Dunkirk,
And the Home Front Show, with doves flying over as we sang,
'White Cliffs of Dover' and that old favourite 'We'll meet again.'

We watched the March of Standards, resplendent in the sun,
Bowed our heads for the Act of Remembrance, Last Post and Kohima,
Joined in when twelve thousand voices repeated 'We Will Remember Them'
And as long as we Veterans live we will.

Her Majesty, The Queen, did us proud that day,
She spoke on behalf of the nation, of the debt we all owe,
To the generation who deserve admiration, respect and thanks
For what they gave in the cause of freedom, all those years ago.

Then it was the Flypast of Vintage Aircraft,
And the dropping of poppies, one for each life given for the nation's future,
The Mall, was thronged, fifty thousand they say, all eager to say 'Thanks'
A magnificent end to a wonderful day.

Mention must be made of the many Police and Military Personnel,
Who were ready with wheelchairs and a friendly helping hand,
To the veterans, now in their eighties and nineties,
Some frail, many with sticks, but so proud to be there.

And 'the hat', what a bargain that turned out to be.
It's a Jacques Vert creation, which suits my granddaughter as well as her Nan.
Despite the difference in ages,
And the cost, would you believe it, just a fiver, from a well-known Charity Shop.

# List of References

*1944 The Battle for Normandy – The Memory* (online), available from http://www. normandie44lamemoire.com.

Anon, *The Wyvern in North West Europe: being a short history of the 43rd Wessex Division, 24 June 1944 - 8 May 1945* (43rd Wessex Division: Germany, 1945).

Badsey, Stephen, *Normandy 1944: Allied Landings and Breakout* (Osprey Publishing Ltd: Oxford, 1990).

Barry, John, *Normandy War Graves Database*.

Belfield, Eversley and Essame, Hubert, *The Battle for Normandy* (Pan Books: London, 1983).

Bernage, Georges, *Bataille de Normadie – Normandy Invasion: 11 Juin - 29 Août* (Editions Heimdal: Bayeux, 1994).

Bernage, Georges, *Enfer sur la cote 112* (Editions Heimdal: Bayeux, 2008).

*Bexhill Observer*, Article 'Brothers recall the wonderful hospitality of generous sisters' (published Friday 26 December 2008).

Bodleian Library, *Instructions for British Servicemen in France 1944* (reprint of original Foreign Office publication) (Bodleian Library: University of Oxford, 2005).

*Bristol Evening Post*, 'Letter from Herbert Haddrell' (published 21 November 1990).

*Bristol Times and Mirror*, 'The Reason Why' (published Friday 30 January 1925).

Brooks, Victor, *The Normandy Campaign: 6 June – 25 August 1944* (Casement Publishing: 2002).

Burton, David, *Bexhill in World War II* (Bexhill Museum Association: Bexhill-on-Sea, 1999).

Caines, Wally G., unpublished diary, Imperial War Museum collection, catalogue no: 306 90/20/1.

Carruthers, Bob and Trew, Simon, *The Normandy Battles* (Cassell: London, 2000).

Cazenave, Stephan, *Chronique de la SS-Pz-AA-10: Formation – Buczacz – Normandie – Arnhem – Poméranie – Halbe* (Editions Heimdal: Bayeux, 2007).

Commonwealth War Graves Commission, *Debt of Honour Register* (online), available from http://www.cwgc.org.

Cooke, D.G., *The Story of Temple Colston School Bristol* (Temple Colston School: Bristol, 1947).

Cowie, Lieutenant-Colonel H.E., *Brief Outline of Events from their Landing in Normandy until 12th July 1944* (unpublished).

Cumberlage, Geoffrey (editor), *BBC War Report: June 6th 1944 – May 1945* (Oxford University Press: Oxford, 1946).

D'Este, Carlo, *Decision in Normandy – The Unwritten Story of Montgomery and the Allied Campaign* (Collins: London, 1983).

Daglish, Ian, *Operation Bluecoat* (Leo Cooper: Barnsley, South Yorkshire, 2003).

de Lannoy, François, *21st Army Group Normandie 1944* (Editions Heimdal: Bayeux, 1994).

Delaforce, Patrick, *The Fighting Wessex Wyverns - From Normandy to Bremerhaven with the 43rd Wessex Division* (Alan Sutton Publishing: Stroud, Gloucestershire, 1994).

Dike, John, *Bristol Blitz Diary* (Redcliffe Press: Bristol, 1982).

Doherty, Richard, *Normandy 1944: The Road to Victory* (Spellmount Publishers: Staplehurst, 2004).

Ellis, Major L.F., *History of the Second World War – Victory in the West Vol. 1 – The Battle of Normandy* (Her Majesty's Stationery Office: London, 1962).

Essame, Major General H., *The 43rd Wessex Division at War, 1944–1945* (William Clowes: London, 1952).

Gazette, 'Letter from Herbert Haddrell published in "Victory in Europe" souvenir supplement' (Dursley, Gloucestershire, 1994).

Grandais, Albert, *La Bataille de Calvados* (Presses de la Cité: Paris, 1973).

Hamilton, Nigel, *Monty: The Making of a General 1887–1942* (McGraw-Hill: London, 1981).

Harmel, Heinz, *In Ehrfurcht die Fahnen Senken: Die 10.SS-Panzer-Division "Frundsberg" im Einsatz vom Juni bis November 1944* (Stenger Historica Publishing: Spotsylvania, Virginia, 1991).

Hastings, Max, *Overlord: D-Day and the Battle for Normandy 1944* (Pan Books: 2004).

Hay, Kenneth, *Personal recollections* (2004).

Henrie, W.F. and Macleod, D.A.D, *The Bangour Story - A History of Bangour Village and General Hospitals* (Aberdeen University Press: Aberdeen, 1991).

Hunt, Eric, *Mont Pinçon* (Leo Cooper: Barnsley, South Yorkshire, 2003).

How, Major J.J., *Hill 112 – cornerstone of the Normandy Campaign* (William Kimber: London, 1984).

Imperial War Museum, *Interview with Herbert Henry Haddrell* (2003).

Keegan, John, *Six Armies in Normandy - From D-Day to the Liberation of Paris* (Penguin Books: Middlesex, 1994).

Kelly's Directories, *Kelly's Directory of Bristol - 1925* (Kelly's Directories Limited: London, 1925).

Kelly's Directories, *Kelly's Directory of Bristol - 1926* (Kelly's Directories Limited: London, 1926).

Kriegstagebuch Nr. 2, 2 SS-Werfer-Abteilung 102 – 24 January to 20 September 1944 (Bundesarchiv Abt. Militärarchiv, Freiburg).

L'Association Odon Cote 112, *La Bataille de la Cote 112 – Un Combat Pour La Liberté, 60 ème anniversaire* (Caen, 2004).

Longden, Sean, *To the Victor the Spoils: D-Day to VE Day, the Reality Behind the Heroism* (Arris Books: Moreton in Marsh, 2005).

Longmate, Norman, *How We Lived Then: A History of Everyday Life During the Second World War* (Pimlico Books: London, 2004).

Medical History from Enlistment to Discharge 1943–1945 of Herbert Henry Haddrell (Ref: M2/265483).

Michaelis, Rolf, *Die 10.SS-Panzer-Division "Frundsberg"* (Schiffer Publishing: 2008).

Ministry of Defence, *Letter given particulars of the military service of Herbert Henry Haddrell* (1987).

Neillands, Robin, *The Battle of Normandy 1944* (Cassell: London, 2002).

Penny, John, *Bristol at War* (Breedon Books Publishing: Derby, 2002).

Place, Timothy Harrison, *Military Training in the British Army, 1940-1944: From Dunkirk to D-Day* (Routledge: Abingdon, Oxon, 2000)

Porter, Frank, *Personal recollections* (2004).

Ripley, Tim, *The Waffen-SS at War: Hitler's Praetorians 1925–1945* (Zenith Press: Osceola, WI, 2004).

Roberts, Lieutenant-Colonel W.G., *Report on the Activities of the 4th Battalion The Dorsetshire Regiment* (unpublished).

Saunders, Tim, *Operation Epsom* (Leo Cooper: Barnsley, South Yorkshire, 2003).

Saunders, Tim, *Hill 112 - Battles of the Odon - 1944* (Leo Cooper: Barnsley, South Yorkshire, 2002).

Stovey, Kenneth, *Personal recollections* (2004).

Swift, Michael and Sharpe, Michael, *Historical Maps of World War II: Europe* (PRC Publishing: London, 2001).

Tieke, Wilhelm, *In the Firestorm of the Last years of the War – II SS-Panzerkorps with the 9. and 10. SS-Divisions "Hohenstaufen" and "Frundsberg"* (J.J. Fedorowicz: Manitoba, Canada, 1999).

Unidentified, *Report on the 4th Dorset's Doings from July 13th to September 26th* (unpublished).

United States War Department, *Handbook on German Military Forces* (Louisiana State University Press: Baton Rouge, Louisiana, 1995).

War Department, Military Intelligence Division, 'Six-Barrel Rocket Weapon (The "Nebelwerfer 41")', *Intelligence Bulletin*, vol. II, no. 3, section II. (November 1943).

War Diary of the 1st Battalion the Worcestershire Regiment, (WO 171/1396), National Archives, Kew, London.

War Diary of the 4th Battalion the Dorset Regiment, (WO 171/1286), National Archives, Kew, London.

War Diary of the 5th Battalion the Dorset Regiment, (WO 171/1287), National Archives, Kew, London.

War Diary of the 7th Battalion the Hampshire Regiment, (WO 171/1306), National Archives, Kew, London.

War Diary of the 9th Royal Tank Regiment, (WO 171/869), National Archives, Kew, London.

War Diary of the No. 10 Casualty Clearing Station, (WO 177/638), National Archives, Kew, London.

War Diary of the 43rd Reconnaissance Regiment, (WO 171/491), National Archives, Kew, London.

War Diary of the 130th Field Ambulance, (WO 177/709), National Archives, Kew, London.

Watkins, G.J.B, *From Normandy to the Weser - The War History of the Fourth Battalion the Dorset Regiment, June 1944 - May 1945* (The Dorset Press: Dorchester, undated).

Williams, Sarah and Rogers, Duncan, *On the Bloody Road to Berlin: Frontline Accounts from North-West Europe & the Eastern Front, 1944–45* (Helion & Company: Solihull, 2005).

Wilmot, Chester, *The Struggle for Europe* (The Reprint Society: London, 1954).

Winstone, Reece, *Bristol Blitzed* (Reece Winstone: Henleaze, Bristol, 1973).

Wood, Lieutenant-Colonel J.L., *Notes, 12th July to 6th August* (unpublished).

Wood, M. and Dugdale, J., *Waffen SS Panzer Units in Normandy 1944: Orders of Battle* (Books International Militaria: 2000).

*The Worcestershire Regiment* (online), available from http://www.worcestershireregiment.com/.

*WW2 The People's War* (online), available from http://www.bbc.co.uk/ww2peopleswar/ user/45/u1740845.shtml.

Zetterling, Niklas, *Normandy 1944: German Military Organization, Combat Power and Organizational Effectiveness* (J.J. Federowicz Publishing: Winnipeg, Manitoba, Canada, 2000)

# Appendix 1

43rd (Wessex) Infantry Division – Order of Battle (6 June 1944 to 5 May 1945)

| | |
|---|---|
| HQ | 43 (Wessex) Infantry Division |
| HQ | 129 Infantry Brigade |
| | 4 Somerset Light Infantry |
| | 4 Wiltshire |
| | 5 Wiltshire |
| HQ | 130 Infantry Brigade |
| | 7 Royal Hampshire |
| | 4 Dorset |
| | 5 Dorset |
| HQ | 214 Infantry Brigade |
| | 7 Somerset Light Infantry |
| | 1 Worcestershire |
| | 5 Duke of Cornwall's Light Infantry |
| Reconnaissance | 43 Reconnaissance Regt (The Gloucestershire Regiment) |
| Machine Gun Battalion | 8 Middlesex |
| Royal Artillery (RA) | 94 Field Regiment |
| | 112 Field Regiment |
| | 179 Field Regiment |
| | 59 Anti-Tank Regiment |
| | 110 L.A.A. Regiment |
| Royal Engineers (RE) | 204 Field Company |
| | 260 Field Company |
| | 553 Field Company |
| | 207 Field Park Company |
| | 13 Bridging Platoon |
| Signals | 43 Wessex Divisional Signals |
| RASC | 504 Company |
| | 505 Company |

|                |                                         |
|----------------|-----------------------------------------|
|                | 54 Company                              |
|                | 506 Company                             |
| RAMC           | 129 Field Ambulance                     |
|                | 130 Field Ambulance                     |
|                | 213 Field Ambulance                     |
|                | 14 Field Dressing Station               |
|                | 15 Field Dressing Station               |
|                | 38 Field Hygiene Section                |
| RAOC           | 43 Ordnance Field Park                  |
|                | 306 Mobile Laundry and Bath Unit        |
| REME           | 129 Infantry Brigade Workshop           |
|                | 130 Infantry Brigade Workshop           |
|                | 214 Infantry Brigade Workshop           |
| PROVOST        | 43 Wessex Division Provost Company RCMP  |
| FIELD SECURITY | 57 Field Security Section               |

# Appendix 2

Transcript of the War Diary of the 4th Battalion the Dorsetshire Regiment: June 1944 – August 1944. The original document is deposited at The National Archives, Kew, London (Reference Number: WO 171/1286).

All units and formations of battalion size and above, and smaller units operating independently, maintained a daily record of operations, intelligence reports and other events, often with appendices of signals and orders. It was kept for each battalion by an appointed junior officer.

Many documents such as war diaries, operational orders and combat reports contain references to locations which look exactly like National Grid references but do not make sense when related to Ordnance Survey National Grid maps. This is because the armed services used a separate military grid, the status of which was top secret. This grid was overprinted on Ordnance Survey maps. The overprint was originally in purple and the grid came to be called the 'purple grid'. The location references in many records of the period make sense only when related to the overprinted maps.

| Place | Date | Hour | Summary of Events |
|---|---|---|---|
| Bexhill | 1 June | | Carrier pigeon with message to Mayor and citizens of DORCHESTER for opening of 'Salute the Soldiers' week. Weather cloudy, slight rain, wind SW. |
| Bexhill | 2 June | | The C.O. addressed the battalion on points brought out by General Montgomery at a recent conference with unit commanders. |
| Bexhill | 3 June | | Fd. Returns of Officers and OR's issued. The ban on troops travelling outside battalion area and six hours notice to move was lifted until 2359 hours. Weather: cloudy with bright intervals, wind South by West |
| Bexhill | 4 June | 1000 | Battalion Church Parade at St Peters Church. Salute at march past by C.O. |
| Bexhill | 5 June | | Inter-company swimming competitions at EGERTON BATHS won by 'C' Company. |

| Bexhill | 5 June | | Unit Personnel and Vehicle Staff Tables (dated 1st June) issued dealing with personnel and vehicles in Advance, Main and Residue parties for move overseas. |
|---|---|---|---|
| Bexhill | 5 June | | Weather: Cloudy. Strong wind, South to West. |
| Bexhill | 6 June | 1030 | 130 Infantry Brigade confirmed today to be 'D'- day. |
| Bexhill | 6 June | 1600 | Battalion to be at 12 hours notice to move until receipt of code-word 'MARY' then to be at six hours notice. |
| Bexhill | 7 June | | Weather: Cloudy with bright intervals – Wind: South West |
| Bexhill | 7 June | | Conference at HASTINGS for all Officers and WOs. Major General THOMAS talked on progress and intentions of A.E.F. 43 Division Intelligence Summaries 1 and 2 issued with Topographical Notes Nos 1 to 6 and 1:25000 Overlay and [Going]? Maps of the area of landings in NORMANDY. These contain notes on German Order of Battle, French Police, attitude of civilians, topography, enemy defences etc. |
| Bexhill | 8 June | | 2 I/C Major L.J. Wood (Officer I/C Vehicle Party) talked to Vehicle Party on move to Embarkation Point and procedure of landing vehicles. |
| Bexhill | 8 June | | Weather: Cloudy, slight drizzle – Wind South to West |
| Bexhill | 9 June | | Weather: Cloudy – Wind South to West |
| Bexhill | 10 June | | Weather: dull, showers and bright intervals – wind: South to West. |
| Bexhill | 10 June | | Fd. Returns of Officers and ORs issued. Battalion received copies of letter from General Eisenhower and armlets for use by civilians employed in France. |
| Bexhill | 11 June | | Battalion Church Parade at ST PETERS CHURCH. Weather: Cloudy, bright intervals – Wind SW to ESE. |
| Bexhill | 12 June | 1230 | Codeword 'MARY' received – Battalion at six hours notice to move from 1800 hrs. |
| Bexhill | 12 June | 1230 | Weather: bright, sunny and warm – Wind NW to West. |
| Bexhill | 13 June | | Weather: Dull, rain, clearing in the evening – Wind SSW to WNW |
| Bexhill | 13 June | 2130 | Battalion Advanced Party, Capt Letson in charge left battalion area. |
| Bexhill | 13 June | | 4 Dorset Unit Security Orders Issued. (Headed '61' Unit Security Orders) |
| Bexhill | 14 June | | Orders received for battalion to move to Marshalling Areas. |

| | | | |
|---|---|---|---|
| Bexhill | 15 June | 0230 | Vehicle Party left battalion area under command of Major L J Wood. |
| Bexhill | 15 June | 0904 | Marching party left Bexhill by train |
| Bexhill | 15 June | 1155 | Vehicle party arrived Marshalling area Camp T1 |
| | 15 June | 1400 | Marching party arrived Marshalling Area Camp C2 and immediately received a hot meal. All Officers attended a conference in the cinema – Subject 'Camp Standing Orders'. |
| | 16 June | 0100 | One OR of Marching party became a casualty through falling in a slit trench during an alert |
| | 17 June | 1620 | Vehicle Party left Camp T1 |
| | 17 June | 1700 | Vehicle Party arrived Embarkation Point – TILBURY |
| | | | During the day Marching party suffered one OR casualty during a football match. 12 Reinforcements (ORs) joined Marching Party. CO attended a conference at 1000 hrs. |
| Tilbury | 17 June | 1900 | Vehicle Party embarked in SS 'OCEAN ANGEL' |
| | 17 June | 2300 | 'OCEAN ANGEL' sailed in convoy from Tilbury. |
| | 18 June | | 'OCEAN ANGEL' in convoy anchored off SHEERNESS. |
| | 18 June | | Both Vehicle and Marching Parties held voluntary Church Parades at sea this morning. |
| | 18 June | 1130 | C.O. attended conference on movement of Marching Parties from CAMP C2. |
| | 19 June | | Vehicle Party sailed into CHANNEL – convoy shelled off DOVER but neither the ship nor personnel were hit – a strong NE gale blowing. |
| | 19 June | 0830 | Marching party left C2 in transport. |
| | 19 June | 1200 | Marching Party embarked in HMTS 'PAMPAS'. |
| | 20 June | 1100 | C.O. attended conference and was shown possible landing places by O.C. Troopship. |
| | 20 June | 2000 | Vehicle party arrived off coast of FRANCE |
| | 21 June | | Vehicle and Marching parties still at sea – Marching Party in Solent |
| | 22 June | | Marching party sailed during night. |
| | 23 June | 0400 | Marching party landed in FRANCE |
| | 23 June | | Marching party concentrated in area 784865 |
| 784865 | 23 June | 2115 | Marching party still in concentration area. 'OCEAN ANGEL' moved closer inshore as sea had now moderated |

| | | | |
|---|---|---|---|
| 784865 | 24 June | | CO attended Corps Conference on future operations. |
| 784865 | 24 June | | One Lloyd Carrier and 7 x 3 ton trucks and White Scout Car were disembarked and reached battalion area. |
| 784865 | 25 June | | During the morning and afternoon CO attended Division and Brigade conferences on Operation 'EPSOM' and C.O. and IO, Lieut. E Andrews went round Coys and put all ranks in the general picture. |
| 784865 | 25 June | 2100 | Battalion O Group – CO gave out orders regarding move to forward Concentration Area. |
| 784865 | 25 June | 2100 | Remainder of Battalion Transport arrived in area |
| 784865 | 25 June | | 4 Dorset Admin Order No.1 (EPSOM) issued dealing with rations. |
| 784865 | 25 June | | Wind SOUTH TO SE – Weather hot and sunny becoming overcast with slight drizzle in the evening |
| 784865 | 26 June | 0815 | Battalion moved out for first 'EPSOM' Concentration Area. |
| 867795 | 26 June | 1000 | Vehicle Group arrived Concentration Area 867795 |
| 867795 | 26 June | 1205 | Marching Troops arrived in area. |
| 867795 | 26 June | 1400 | News received that operation going well. |
| 867795 | 26 June | 1800 | CO and IO attended O Group at Brigade HQ on further movements of Brigade – 43 Division to take over covering position from 3 Canadian Division. |
| 867795 | 27 June | 0700 | Battalion 'R' Group – CO, IO Company Commanders and specialist Platoon Commanders moved off for new area. |
| 867795 | 27 June | | Weather this morning showery with sunny intervals, roads greasy. |
| 867795 | 27 June | 0830 | 'R' Group arrived new area PUTOT-EN-BESSIN 9072 and were taken round Company areas by representatives of Regiment de la Chaudiere. |
| 902724 | 27 June | 1330 | Whole of battalion less 'B' Echelon concentrated in PUTOT area and battalion took over positions. Transport was held up by heavy traffic on roads. During the afternoon the unit settled in amidst very muddy and showery conditions. 2 I/C Anti Tank Platoon Lieut. McFee whilst examining an enemy grave discovered a booby trap attached to a German rifle and set it off from a distance. This was the first booby trap encountered by the battalion. News was received |

| | | | |
|---|---|---|---|
| | | | that Lt Col. [John Winn] Atherton the Battalions old 2 I/C had been killed in action in CHEUX area. |
| 902724 | 27 June | 2145 | C.O. held an 'O' Group at Battalion HQ dealing with latest developments. |
| 902724 | 28 June | 0900 | C.O. held conference of Company Commanders on general situation. Battalion was to have been relieved by a battalion of 32 Guards Brigade but this was altered. |
| 902724 | 28 June | | Weather cloudy with sunny intervals |
| 902724 | 28 June | 1230 | Battalion ordered to stand by for move to River Odon bridgehead area, where 130 Brigade was to have taken over from 159 Brigade. CO sent IO forward to recce a route from battalion area. |
| 902724 | 28 June | 1330 | C.O. held 'O' Group and gave warning order for move forward. Battalion at half hours notice to move. |
| 902724 | 28 June | 1530 | Brigade informed battalion that move is unlikely today. Battalion at one hours notice. |
| 902724 | 28 June | 2000 | C.O. visited Company localities |
| 902724 | 28 June | 2230 | Battalion stood down for next 10 hours at one hours notice from 0800/29 June. |
| 902724 | 29 June | 0930 | C.O. held 'O' Group and told Company Commanders of general situation. Battalion still at one hours notice to move. |
| 902724 | 29 June | 1330 | Orders from Brigade that battalion is to be prepared to move at 1500 hrs |
| 902724 | 29 June | 1450 | C.O. held 'O' Group – gave orders for move to new area to take over from 5th DCLI |
| 902724 | 29 June | 1530 | C.O. accomplished by IO, Company Commanders and Platoon Commanders of S Company left for new area. |
| 909669 | 29 June | 1620 | Battalion 'R' Group arrived in 5th DCLIs area and Company Commanders were taken round Company localities by representatives of the 5th DCLI. |
| 909669 | 29 June | 1840 | Marching troops arrived and were in process of taking over when news was received of an enemy counter-attack with tanks. The C.O. immediately placed 'B' and 'C' Companies under command of 5th DCLI with Major G. Connor at Battalion HQ to act as liaison officer. These companies with the Anti Tank, Mortar and Carrier platoons doubled up with their opposite numbers. Meanwhile the C.O. held 'A' and 'D' |

| | | | |
|---|---|---|---|
| | | | Companies as a counter-attack force to work with a squadron of Churchill tanks and concentrated them in the orchards at HAUT DU BOSC 9066. Little reliable information was available about the whereabouts of the enemy. The area was mortared and shelled, the battalion suffered seven casualties, 1 OR killed and 6 ORs wounded. The mortars in conjunction with those of the DCLI registered on WOOD 902666. |
| 909669 | 29 June | 2000 | The situation was now very confused, parties of ROYAL SCOTS and RSF who had been SOUTH of our position began to arrive in the village and tank squadrons of 11 Armoured Division formed up in area of high ground 911660. The tanks moved off SOUTH-WEST along the CHEUX-NOYERS road. |
| 909669 | 29 June | 2200 | The CO went forward in his carrier to find out the true situation in front. On arriving in area 900657 he discovered the survivors of the ROYAL SCOTS and RSF under their respective C.O.s forming an all road defensive area astride the road. These were well supported by tanks in their area and seemed satisfied with their position so the CO returned along the road towards CHEUX. On the way he met 'D' and 'A' Companies whom he had ordered to move up before leaving the village. He now ordered them to return and double up with their corresponding DCLI Companies. |
| 909669 | 30 June | 0130 | 5th DCLIs moved out and battalion took over the area. The weather was cloudy and stormy. |
| 909669 | 30 June | | During the night the battalion received a hot meal. Two ORs of RSF brought in a Polish prisoner whom they had captured at COLLEVILLE 9265 and identification of 4 Company 20 SS Panzer Grenadiers was obtained. |
| 909669 | 30 June | 0420 | The battalion stood to in their slit-trenches. |
| 909669 | 30 June | | The early part of morning was spent by the CO in teeing up his fire-plan, paying particular attention to the Anti-Tank plan. |
| 909669 | 30 June | 1100 | 5th Dorsets and 7th Hants began to arrive in CHEUX area. Brigadier Leslie held an O Group at Battalion HQ stressing need for intensified observation and a sound Anti-Tank plan. |

| | | | |
|---|---|---|---|
| 909669 | 30 June | 1200 | Battalion IO recced and sited an additional I Sec OP (one had already been established in Battalion HQ area). C.O. ordered 'B' and 'C' Companies to establish Company Ops. Weather: Cloudy with bright interval – Wind: SW. |
| 909669 | 30 June | 2000 | Several hundreds of LANCASTER and HALIFAX heavy bombers were observed to be carrying out a large scale air-raid SW of battalion area, believed in area NOYERS-VILLERS BOCAGE. |
| 909669 | 30 June | 2130 | CO visited Company and Platoon positions. |
| 909669 | 30 June | 2230 | Battalion stood to in their slit trenches. |
| 909669 | 30 June | 2315 | Stand down. |
| 909669 | 1 July | | Fd Returns of Officers and O.R.s issued |
| 909669 | 2 July | 0420 | Battalion stood to till daylight. |
| 909669 | 2 July | | During the morning troops in front of Battalion (44 Brigade) were relieved by troops of 53rd Division. The C.O. visited Companies and the Battalion OP at 905661. The brigade Commander visited Battalion and A Company were moved to area 906663 where they dug in. Trace of battalion area made. The Brigadier again visited the Battalion HQ at about 1600 hrs and it was decided to move 'A' Company to another area. The C.O. accompanied the brigadier to the area and platoons of A Company were redisposed. |
| 909669 | 2 July | 1730 | Battalion received Warning Orders to move in four hours. |
| 909669 | 2 July | 1920 | Representatives of RWF (53rd Division) arrived to recce area before relief. |
| 909669 | 2 July | 2100 | Relieving troops arrived in battalion area. |
| 909669 | 2 July | 2200 | Relief completed battalion moved out. |
| 917681 | 2 July | 2300 | Battalion concentrated around area 917681. |
| 917681 | 2 July | 2359 | Hot drink issued to all ranks. Weather – Rain – Wind – SW. |
| 917681 | 3 July | 0700 | Battalion still in Concentration Area. |
| 917681 | 3 July | | Heavy rain this morning – Wind SW. |
| 917681 | 3 July | 1400 | CO went to 130 Brigade HQ for a conference on the projected attack in which battalion is to take part. |
| 917681 | 3 July | 1509 | A number of shells fell in battalion area, three casualties resulted – 2 killed [Privates Loosmore and Vater] and 1 injured. |

| | | | |
|---|---|---|---|
| 917681 | 3 July | 1630 | CO returned from Brigade HQ and gave talk to all Officers on forthcoming operation. |
| 917681 | 3 July | 1700 | Weather now cleared but still cloudy – Wind WEST |
| 917681 | 3 July | 1730 | The CO and OC 5th Dorsets accompanied by the Battalion IO set off for area 9465 to recce ground over which operation is to take place. The general plan is to be as followed:- 129 Brigade are holding area 9464, the battalion with the rest of 130 Brigade are to break out SOUTH and EAST supported by tanks. Battalion's first objective to be ETERVILLE 9864 and consolidation area SOUTH of MALTOT 9462 which is to be captured by 7 Hampshire Regiment. |
| 917681 | 3 July | 2105 | C.O. returned from recce |
| 917681 | 3 July | 2130 | Major Holder, Squadron Commander of the supporting tanks visited C.O. and discussed the operation with him. |
| 917681 | 4 July | 0700 | CO accompanied by the Adjutant went to an 'O' Group at 130 Brigade HQ. |
| 917681 | 4 July | 0842 | Enemy shells dropped in battalion area. |
| 917681 | 4 July | 0920 | C.O. and Adjutant returned to Battalion HQ. |
| 917681 | 4 July | 0949 | CO., IO., S Company Commander and Pioneer Platoon Commander left for area TRETTE POUX on recce. |
| 917681 | 4 July | 1320 | COs party returned from the recce. |
| 917681 | 4 July | 1530 | The CO told all Officers the general outline of the plan of attack. |
| 917681 | 4 July | 1630 | The CO and officers down to Platoon Commanders left for TRETTE POUX where the orders for attack were given by CO and Rifle Company Officers went forward to an OP manned by 5th DCLIs and studied the ground. Orders: – 'A' Company to be right forward Company, 'B' Company on left followed by 'C' Company on right, 'D' Company on left. Advanced Battalion HQ to be established on ridge NE of ETERVILLE with Rear HQ dug in NORTH of the road at TRETTE POUX. Supporting Tanks and SP 17 pounders to be forward of 'B' Company and on the left to give covering fire. One troop of 17 pounders to cover FUP area 968649. Forward Companies to push through village stopping only to overcome strong points or serious opposition. Companies to consolidate as follows: 'A' Company area 984639; 'B' Company |

| | | | |
|---|---|---|---|
| | | | area 986640: 'C' Company area ORCHARDS 681642; 'D' Company area Point 52 – 686643. |
| 917681 | 4 July | 1700 | Party of reinforcements arrived at Battalion HQ. |
| 917681 | 4 July | 2023 | COs Recce party returned |
| 917681 | 4 July | 2024 | UX Shell landed D Company lines |
| 917681 | 4 July | 2230 | Warning orders received from Brigade – attack post-poned – move in 36 hours to relieve a battalion of 159 Brigade across RIVER ODON. |
| 917681 | 5 July | 0919 | CO accompanied by IO and I Sgt left to recce new battalion area. |
| 917681 | 5 July | 1030 | CO's party arrived 159 Brigade HQ and were told that they would relieve battalion of HEREFORD Regt in area 934628. Orders sent back to battalion that recce party down to Section Commanders would RV at 159 Brigade HQ 929641 at 1500 hrs. CO and party went down over ODON and recced area. |
| 934628 | 5 July | 1630 | Battalion Recce parties arrived and were taken round localities by representatives of HEREFORDS |
| 917681 | 5 July | 1900 | Battalion 'O' Group: orders given for move. |
| 917681 | 5 July | 2045 | Marching Party left for new area |
| 917681 | 5 July | 2130 | Vehicle Party moved out. Whilst passing through TOURVILLE [Tourmauvile] the road was shelled but neither damage nor casualties were sustained. |
| 933628 | 6 July | 0045 | Battalion established in new area. |
| 933628 | 6 July | 0450 | Battalion stood to in positions. |
| 933628 | 6 July | 0530 | Battalion stood down. |
| 933628 | 6 July | 1130 | Mortars registered D/F tasks. |
| 933628 | 6 July | 1445 | C.O. visited Companies. |
| 933628 | 6 July | 1515 | Battalion area mortared. 3 injured. 1 jeep and 1 carrier. |
| 933628 | 6 July | 1800 | Details of patrols sent to Brigade. |
| 933628 | 6 July | 2330 | 'B' company patrol left area under command Lt Cottle. |
| 933628 | 7 July | 0100 | Patrol 'D' Company under command of Lt Andrews left battalion area. |
| 933628 | 7 July | 0200 | Battalion Stood To in slit trenches. |
| 933628 | 7 July | 0230 | 'B' Company patrol returned. Contacted enemy on way back. Six ORs missing. One wounded. |
| 933628 | 7 July | 0400 | 'D' Company patrol returned. 3 killed. 4 injured, one died from wounds. [Lance-Corporal Dury and Privates Rayment, Smith and Stroud] |

| | | | |
|---|---|---|---|
| 933628 | 7 July | 0300 | 'A' Company patrol returned. (Lt Knight) |
| 933628 | 7 July | 0300 | 50% Battalion Stood Down. |
| 933628 | 7 July | 0430 | Battalion Stood To. |
| 933628 | 7 July | 0530 | Battalion Stood Down. |
| 933628 | 7 July | 0645 | Sgt Northover & Sgt Morgan, 2 'I' ORs and 2 snipers went out to take up O.P. in area 934621 |
| 933628 | 7 July | 1100 | Sgt Morgan and 1 sniper O.R. returned. O.P. Group attacked. 3 Int: ORs missing. |
| 933628 | 7 July | 1330 | M.O. Sgt went forward to enemy lines to contact wounded. |
| 933628 | 7 July | 1700 | Royal Scot relief recce party's arrived. |
| 933628 | 7 July | 1930 | Warning Order to move. |
| 933628 | 7 July | 2230 | Battalion Stood Down. |
| 933628 | 7 July | 2300 | Standing patrol reported no enemy activity except from snipers |
| 933628 | 7 July | 2330 | Battalion Stood Down. |
| 933628 | 8 July | 0030 | Double Stand To (Royal Scots & Dorset) |
| 933628 | 8 July | 0130 | Battalion Stood Down and prepared to move. |
| 933628 | 8 July | 0200 | Battalion transport moved. |
| 933628 | 8 July | 0245 | Marching troops moved. |
| 933628 | 8 July | 0300 | Battalion transport arrived new area. |
| 933628 | 8 July | 0500 | Marching troops arrived new area. |
| 933628 | 8 July | 0500 | Hot breakfast meal. |
| 933628 | 8 July | 1425 | C.O. and I.O. went to Brigade. |
| 933628 | 8 July | | C.O. and I.O. returned. |
| 901693 | 9 July | | Battalion resting. |
| 901693 | 9 July | 0900 | C.O., I.O., Company Commanders plus platoon commanders of 'S' Company proceeded on recce of new area and C.O. issued orders for forthcoming attack on Éterville. |
| 901693 | 9 July | 1500 | Recce party returned. |
| 937764 | 10 July | 0115 | Battalion moved to concentration area 937646 |
| 937646 | 10 July | 0500 | Hot meal served before moving up to F.U.P. |
| 968648 | 10 July | 0530 | Battalion moved to F.U.P. 968648 |
| 968648 | 10 July | 0620 | F.U.P. bombed by mortars. Attack commenced A & B Companies forward with C & D Companies in reserve. Supporting tanks covered right flank. |

| | | | |
|---|---|---|---|
| 968648 | 10 July | 0745 | Objective taken Companies consolidated in areas – A Company 984639. B Company 986640. C Company 981642. D Company 986643. Forward Battalion H.Q. area of church 982643. Rear Battalion H.Q. dug in at north of road Trette Poux 9664. Battalion being heavily mortared. Considerable casualties. |
| 968648 | 10 July | 1345 | Battalion was relieved by Cameronians. 26 P.W. were handed over to them. |
| 976642 | 10 July | 1400 | Battalion reorganised in the area 976642 in preparation to assist 7th Hampshire Regiment in Maltot 9862. |
| 976642 | 10 July | 1445 | C.O.'s 'O' Group and Orders. |
| 976635 | 10 July | 1535 | Battalion formed up at F.U.P. 976635 |
| 976635 | 10 July | 1620 | Attack commenced with tanks in support. |
| 976635 | 10 July | 1645 | Objective gained. |
| 976635 | 10 July | 1700 | Consolidation by Infantry. |
| 973641 | 10 July | 2030 | Battalion was forced to withdraw after having suffered heavy casualties by dug in tanks. Battalion withdrew through 7 S.L.I. and took up position at 973641. |
| 973641 | 10 July | 2130 | Heavy shelling on battalion area by artillery and mortars. 1 casualty. |
| 974635 | 11 July | 0530 | Battalion moved position to 974635 where the L.O.B's rejoined unit. Considerable mortar shelling throughout the day. No casualties. |
| 974635 | 11 July | 1845 | Battalion relieved by 5th Dorsets. |
| 920651 | 11 July | 2030 | Battalion arrived at rest area 920651 to reorganize. |
| 920651 | 12 July | 1030 | 12 reinforcements arrived from 33 R.H.U. |
| 920651 | 12 July | 1900 | Heavy shelling in battalion area. No casualties. |
| 920651 | 12 July | 2030 | Lt Col. H.E. Cowie left the battalion and the 2 I/O Major L.J. Wood assumed command. |
| 920651 | 13 July | 1245 | Battalion area shelled. 3 casualties including M.O. & Padre. |
| 920651 | 13 July | 1347 | Battalion area shelled. 1 x 3 tonner set on fire. |
| 920651 | 13 July | 1725 | Reinforcements arrived. 7 Officers & 338 O.R's from 33 R.H.U. |
| 920651 | 14 July | 0930 | C.O.'s 'O' Group. |
| 920651 | 14 July | 1100 | C.O. attended Brigade conference |
| 920651 | 14 July | 1410 | C.O. returned from Brigade. |
| 920651 | 14 July | 1548 | Battalion area shelled. 1 casualty. |

| | | | |
|---|---|---|---|
| 920651 | 14 July | 1650 | C.O's 'O' Group. |
| 920651 | 14 July | 1735 | Guide party left for forward area where battalion was to relieve the 1st Worcs Regiment in holding sector north of Maltot 9862 |
| 920651 | 14 July | 1950 | Battalion area shelled. 3 casualties. |
| 920651 | 14 July | 2135 | Marching personnel left for new area |
| 9663 | 14 July | 2315 | Battalion arrived at new location 9663 |
| 967633 | 15 July | | Battalion consolidated in new position. Battalion HQ at 967663 |
| 967633 | 15 July | 2100 | C.O.'s 'O' Group |
| 967633 | 15 July | 2145 | Attack on our right flank by 15th (S) Division. Heavy shelling all night. |
| 967633 | 16 July | 0525 | Patrol under Cpl. Hall ('I' Section) went forward to recce possible O.P. for observing orchard 982624. |
| 967633 | 16 July | 0745 | Patrol returned, unable to locate orchard owing to thick smoke. |
| 967633 | 16 July | | Intermittent shelling from enemy all morning. |
| 967633 | 16 July | 1830 | Visit by Brigadier. |
| 967633 | 16 July | 1900 | Tiger tank knocked out by our Anti-tank Regiment. |
| 967633 | 16 July | 2200 | Enemy planes over battalion area. Positions to our rear bombed. Propaganda leaflets dropped. 'A' Company 5th Dorsets came under our command. |
| 967633 | 17 July | | Shelling and mortaring continued from both sides. |
| 967633 | 17 July | 1835 | 3 Officers reinforcements arrived. |
| 967633 | 18 July | 0820 | Mortar bomb exploded in Battalion H.Q. wounding the C.O. Lt Col. L.J. Wood and the I.O. Both admitted to 20th General Hospital, Bayeux. |
| 967633 | 18 July | | 2 Officers posted from 32 R.H.U. |
| 967633 | 18 July | 0900 | 2 I/C Major Tilly assumed command of the battalion. |
| 967633 | 18 July | 1830 | Brigadier visited Battalion H.Q. |
| 967633 | 18 July | 2000 | C.O. visited Company areas. |
| 966638 | 18 July | 2200 | Battalion H.Q. moved back 300 yards to new position 966638 |
| 966638 | 18 July | | Shelling and mortaring throughout the night |
| 966638 | 19 July | 1100 | Brigadier visited Battalion H.Q. |
| 966638 | 19 July | 1430 | 'A' Company warned to take over the Company position from 5th Dorsets. |
| 966638 | 19 July | 1700 | Reinforcements arrived from 'A' Echelon. |

| | | | |
|---|---|---|---|
| 966638 | 20 July | 0030 | 'A' Company relieved company of 5th Dorsets in area 971635 |
| 966638 | 20 July | 1130 | Brigadier and Brigade I.O. visited Battalion H.Q. |
| 966638 | 20 July | 1500 | C.O.'s 'O' Group. |
| 966638 | 20 July | 1700 | 'B' Company moved their position slightly forward to 973628 |
| 966638 | 20 July | 2315 | Heavily armed patrol from 'A' Company sent out to investigate houses at 983624 |
| 966638 | 21 July | 0145 | 2 PW brought to Battalion H.Q. by 'B' Company. Identified as from 10 S.S. Panzer Division. One speaking very good English gave us very valuable information. Passed on to Division. |
| 966638 | 21 July | 1500 | Brigadier and Brigade I.O. visited Battalion H.Q. |
| 966638 | 21 July | 1700 | Barrage by Brigade mortars and artillery commenced on tasks. For preparation of attack by 129 Infantry Brigade. |
| 966638 | 21 July | 1730 | Attack on Maltot by 129 Brigade started. |
| 966638 | 22 July | 0100 | Attack on our immediate right by 1 Worcs commenced, objective being high ridge in front of our position. |
| 966638 | 22 July | 1630 | Visit by Brigadier to Battalion H.Q. |
| 966638 | 23 July | | Intermittent shelling and mortaring throughout day. |
| 966638 | 24 July | 1100 | C.O. issued orders for Companies to hold themselves in readiness to be relieved possibly tonight. |
| 966638 | 24 July | 1430 | Visit by Divisional Commander. |
| 966638 | 24 July | 1630 | Brigadier visited Battalion H.Q. |
| 966638 | 24 July | 2240 | 1 bomb dropped by enemy aircraft near 'S' Company area 967640. 1 O.R. killed 1 Officer wounded. |
| 966638 | 25 July | 0800 | Recce party of relieving unit met at Brigade H.Q. and brought out to recce our area |
| 966638 | 25 July | 1000 | Visit by our own and relieving units Brigadier. |
| 966638 | 25 July | 1130 | Orders issued for movement back to rest area. Routes recceed. |
| 966638 | 25 July | 1400 | Marshalling party and vehicles left for rest area. |
| 966638 | 25 July | 1900 | Company representatives left concentration area. |
| 966638 | 26 July | 0115 | Operational role handed over to R.W.F. and battalion move to concentration area Bas de Mouen 9465 |
| 966638 | 26 July | 0220 | Marching personnel arrived concentration area. Battalion rested. Had hot meal at 0730 |

| | | | |
|---|---|---|---|
| 966638 | 26 July | 0930 | Battalion left concentration area. Passed Division S.P. at 1015 hrs. Divisional Commander took salute at 1025 hrs. |
| 966638 | 26 July | 1415 | Battalion arrived at rest area – Condé-sur-Seulles |
| 966638 | 26 July | 1930 | C.O. issued orders to all officers re. programme at rest area |
| 966638 | 27 July | | Battalion spent day in general administration. |
| 966638 | 28 July | 1400 | Divisional Commander addressed all troops in the Brigade. |
| 966638 | 29 July | 0730 | Warning order received for battalion to be ready to move by 1200 hrs. |
| 966638 | 29 July | 0900 | I.O. went to Brigade to collect maps and orders |
| 966638 | 29 July | 1330 | Battalion moved off in T.C.V.'s for new area |
| 723604 | 29 July | 1745 | Battalion arrived new location 723604 and dug in. |
| 723604 | 29 July | | Slight enemy mortaring throughout night. |
| 723604 | 29 July | 1945 | C.O. 'O' Group. |
| 723604 | 29 July | 2100 | C.O. visited Brigade for orders. |
| 723604 | 30 July | 0130 | C.O. 'O' Group. It is intended that the battalion will attack and capture La Londe 7157 and if successful push on to Cahagnes 7356 |
| 723604 | 30 July | 0515 | C.O. with Company Commanders had last final recce to view the ground over which attack was to take place |
| 723604 | 30 July | 0920 | Battalion moved up to F.U.P. |
| 723604 | 30 July | 1000 | Attack postponed owing to 5th Dorsets meeting stiff opposition. |
| 723604 | 30 July | 1500 | Brigadier's conference. |
| 723604 | 30 July | 1800 | Battalion reformed approx. 400 yards in area of F.U.P. and stayed there the night. |
| 723604 | 31 July | 0500 | Battalion moved forward to area 713588 had breakfast and dug in. |
| 723604 | 31 July | 0900 | Patrols from 'A' Company sent forward to orchards 7157 |
| 723604 | 31 July | 0930 | Brigadier visited Battalion H.Q. |
| 723604 | 31 July | 1100 | 2 officers and 46 O.R.'s P.W dealt with and sent back to Div. Cage. |
| 723604 | 31 July | 1500 | Battalion H.Q. moved to area 716582. Companies pushing forward. |
| 723604 | 31 July | 1630 | Battalion moved forward with Battalion H.Q. established at house 732599 |
| 723604 | 31 July | 1900 | Companies cleared orchards 735575 and Battalion H.Q. moved up to 734581 |
| 734581 | 01 Aug | 0550 | 2 forward O.P.'s manned by snipers and Int. Sec. |

| | | | |
|---|---|---|---|
| 734581 | 01 Aug | 1145 | Representative from Green Howards (50 Division) visited Battalion H.Q. Battalion warned possibility of move in near future. |
| 734581 | 01 Aug | 2000 | C.O. went to Brigade for orders. |
| 734581 | 01 Aug | 2115 | Warning order received for battalion to concentrate in area 728586 and prepare to push forward on a thrust line to Ondefontaine 7849 |
| 734581 | 01 Aug | 2330 | E.A. [Enemy Aircraft] bombed very close to battalion area. No casualties |
| 728586 | 01 Aug | 0115 | Battalion moved off and proceeded at a steady pace in S.E. direction. |
| 728586 | 02 Aug | 0600 | Battalion scout car blown up and adjutant and 1 NCO killed. |
| 728586 | 02 Aug | 0915 | Leading Company (A) encountered mines and machine guns near Jurques 7451. Patrols pushed forward and battalion moved on at a slow pace against stiff opposition. |
| 758505 | 02 Aug | 1700 | Battalion H.Q. established at 758505 and Companies forward on ridge |
| 758505 | 02 Aug | 1915 | C.O. visited Brigade H.Q. |
| 758505 | 02 Aug | | Major Tilly (2 I/C) assumed command of the battalion in absence of C.O. who returned to 'B' Echelon for a rest. |
| 758505 | 02 Aug | 2230 | Battalion stood to until 0130 hrs. |
| 758505 | 03 Aug | 0410 | Battalion stood to until 0550 hrs. |
| 758505 | 03 Aug | | Shelling and mortaring throughout morning. |
| 758505 | 03 Aug | 1400 | Battalion attacked with the intention of clearing woods to south of Ondefontaine 7849 and also to occupy village. |
| 758505 | 03 Aug | 1615 | Enemy counter-attacked our fwd. positions and battalion was pinned down. Battalion H.Q. personnel and remainder of S Company went forward to give support. |
| 758505 | 03 Aug | 1800 | Counter-attack beaten off and Companies took up original positions. |
| 758505 | 03 Aug | 2130 | 1 Officer and 21 O.R.'s arrived as reinforcements. |
| 758505 | 03 Aug | | Mortaring and shelling throughout night. |

Following their involvement at La Bigne and Ondefontaine on 3 August, the 4th Dorsets moved on to Mont Pinçon, seeing action at Arnhem, Geilenkirchen, the Reichswald Forest, and Glinstedt and Augustendorf, before becoming part of the Army of Occupation in Germany.

# Appendix 3

Campaign medals awarded to Herbert Henry Haddrell:

The 1939–1945 Star was awarded for six months service
(two months for operational aircrew) between
3 September 1939 and 15 August 1945 under operational
command.

The France and Germany Star was granted for entry into
operational service on land from 6 June 1944, in France,
Belgium, Holland or Germany, until 8 May 1945, the date
of the end of active hostilities in Europe.

The Defence Medal was awarded
for three years' service in the United
Kingdom between 3 September
1939 and 2 September 1945, or
six months overseas in a non-
operational area subject to aerial
attack.

Reverse of the Defence Medal.

The War Medal 1939–1945 was
awarded to all persons serving
full-time in the Armed Forces
for twenty-eight days between
3 September 1939 and
2 September 1945.

Reverse of the War Medal
1939–1945.

# Appendix 4

Documents:

A page from Bert's 'Medical History from Enlistment to Discharge' containing details of his injuries and treatment.

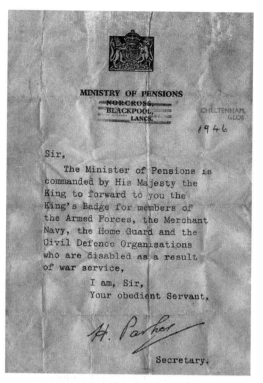

The Minister of Pensions sent an accompanying letter to recipients of the King's Badge.

Bert Haddrell's Army discharge certificate inserted in his AB64 (Army Book 64), issued at Infantry Record Office, Exeter, 4 June 1945.

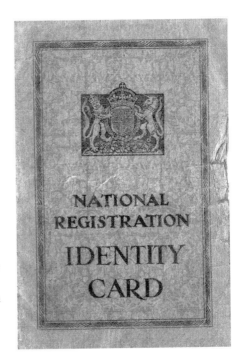

Bert's National Registration Identity Card. The government introduced National Registration Identity Cards under the National Registration Act 1939. All civilians, including children, had to carry an identity card at all times to show who they were and where they lived.

The identity card gave the owner's name and address and unique National Registration number. The local registration office stamped the card to make it valid. Identification was necessary in case families became separated in the event of bombing or if the children were evacuated to another part of the country. People also had to produce their identity card along with their ration book when they were claiming their share of food or clothes. The British wartime identity card scheme was abolished in 1952.

# Appendix 5

An article, on the German *Nebelwerfer* rocket weapon, taken from the November 1943 issue of the American Army Intelligence Bulletin. The following article is war-time information on enemy equipment published for Allied soldiers:

SIX-BARREL ROCKET WEAPON
(THE 'NEBELWERFER 41')

1. Introduction

Whenever the fortunes of the German Army take a new turn for the worse, Nazi prop-agandists attempt to encourage the people of the Reich – and influence public opinion in neutral countries – by spreading rumours of new and formidable developments in German ordnance. Recently the Nazis have been releasing propaganda declaring that spectacular results are being achieved with the German six-barrel rocket projector known as the Nebelwerfer (smoke mortar) 41. Actually, this is not a particularly new weapon. Its name, moreover, is extremely misleading. In the first place, the Nebelwerfer 41 is not a mortar at all, and, in the second place, it can accommodate both gas-charged and high-explosive projectiles, as well as smoke projectiles.

It would be just as foolish to discount the German claims 100 percent as it would be to accept them unreservedly. Although fire from the Nebelwerfer 41 is relatively inaccurate, one of the weapon's chief assets appears to be the concussion effect of its high-explosive projectiles, which is considerable when the weapon's six barrels are fired successively, 1 second apart. The high-explosive round contains 5 pounds of explosive; this is compara-ble – in weight, at least – to the high-explosive round used in the U. S. 105-mm howitzer.

In view of the mass of misleading information which has been circulated regarding the Nebelwerfer 41 – or, as the Germans sometimes call it, the Do-Gerät – it is hoped that junior officers and enlisted men will find the following discussion both timely and profitable.

2. Description

The Nebelwerfer 41 is a six-barrelled (non-rotating) tubular projector, with barrels 3 to 3 1/2 feet long and 160mm in diameter. The projector is mounted on a rubber-tired artillery chassis with a split trail.

German six-barrel rocket projector (side view).

There is no rifling; the projectiles are guided by three rails, each about 1/3-inch high, which run down the inside of the barrels. This reduces the caliber to approximately 150mm.

The barrels are open-breeched, and the propellant is slow-burning black powder (14 pounds set behind the nose cap). This propellant generates gas through 26 jets set at an angle. As a result, the projectiles rotate and travel at an ever-increasing speed, starting with the rocket blast. The burster, which is in the rear two-sevenths of the projectile, has its own time fuze. The range is said to be about 7,760 yards.

The barrels are fired electrically, from a distance. They are never fired simultaneously, since the blast from six rockets at once undoubtedly would capsize the weapon. The order of fire is fixed at 1–4–6–2–3–5.

The sighting and elevating mechanisms are located on the left-hand side of the barrels, immediately over the wheel, and are protected by a light-metal hinged box cover, which is raised when the weapon is to be used.

Each barrel has a metal hook at the breech to hold the projectile in place, and a sparking device to ignite the rocket charge. This sparker can be turned to one side to permit loading and then turned back so that the 'spark jump' is directed to an electrical igniter placed in one of 24 rocket blast openings located on the projectile, about one-third of the way up from the base. About one-third of the length of the projectile extends below the breech of the weapon.

German six-barrel rocket projector (rear view).

The projectile itself resembles a small torpedo – without propeller or tail fins. The base is flat, with slightly rounded edges. The rocket jets are located about one-third of the way up the projectile from the base, and encircle the casing. The jets are at an angle with the axis of the projectile so as to impart rotation in flight, in 'turbine' fashion.

The propelling charge is housed in the forward part of the rocket. A detonating fuze is located in the base of the projectile to detonate the high-explosive or smoke charge. In this way, on impact, the smoke or high explosive is set off above ground when the nose of the projectile penetrates the soil.

3. Note on Operation

The following note on the operation of the Nebelwerfer 41 is reproduced from the German Army periodical Die Wehrmacht. It is believed to be substantially correct.

The Nebelwerfer 41, or Do-Gerät, is unlimbered and placed in position by its crew of four men. As soon as the protective coverings have been removed, the projector is ready to be aimed and loaded. The ammunition is attached to the right and to the left of the projector, within easy reach, and the shells are introduced two at a time, beginning with the lower barrels and continuing upward. Meanwhile, foxholes deep enough to conceal a man in standing position have been dug about 10 to 15 yards to the side and rear of the projector. The gunners remain in these foxholes while the weapon is being fired by electrical ignition. Within 10 seconds a battery can fire 36 projectiles. These make a droning pipe-organ sound as they leave the barrels, and, while in flight, leave a trail of smoke. After a salvo has been fired, the crew quickly returns to its projectors and reloads them.

4. How the German Army Uses It

The following statements have been made by a high-ranking German Army officer, and may be accepted as an authoritative expression of German ideas concerning the employment of this weapon.

Units of Nebeltruppen (smoke-laying troops) are organized as rocket-projector regiments (Werferregimenter), which are fully motorized and therefore extremely mobile. A rocket-projector regiment is divided into battalions and batteries, like those of the artillery. Since rocket-projector regiments are capable of playing a decisive part in battle, they may be concentrated at strategically important points along a front. The organization of a rocket-projector regiment is much like that of a motorized artillery regiment; organizationally, the motor vehicles and signal equipment of both are also much the same. Since the projector units usually are kept close behind the forward infantry line, their batteries may also be equipped with antitank guns. Because of the light construction of the projectors, a 3-ton prime mover is sufficient for traction purposes, and can also carry the gun crew and some of the ammunition.

The Nebelwerfer 41 can fire three different types of projectiles: high-explosive shells, incendiary projectiles, and smoke projectiles.

The high-explosive shells include those with supersensitive fuzes and those with delayed-action fuzes. The latter can penetrate reinforced cover. Because of their fragmentation and concussion effect, high-explosive shells are used primarily against personnel. It has been found that the concussion has not only been great enough to kill personnel, but occasionally has caused field fortifications and bunkers to collapse.

The incendiary projectiles are psychologically effective, and under favorable conditions can start field and forest fires. The smoke projectiles are used to form smoke screens or smoke zones.

Rocket-projector troops are employed as battalion and regimental units, in keeping with their task of destroying hostile forces by concentrated fire. One of the advantages of the Nebelwerfer 41 is that it can mass its projectiles on a very small target area. By means of a shrewd disposition of the batteries, a carefully planned communication system, and a large number of observation posts with advanced observers, the infantry can assure for itself manoeuvrability and a concentration of its fire power upon the most important points. Projectors are placed well toward the front – almost without exception, at points forward of the artillery – so that they will be able to eliminate hostile command posts, destroy hostile positions, and even repulse sudden attacks effectively. The firing positions of the projectors are always carefully built up so that the weapons can give strong support to the infantry.

# Appendix 6

The Commonwealth War Graves Commission's 'Debt of Honour Register' lists twenty-five men of the 4th Dorsets killed on 3 August 1944. Amongst that number are members of No. 2 Platoon killed by the same bombardment that wounded Bert that summer day.

| Name | Rank | Number | Age | War Cemetery |
|---|---|---|---|---|
| Ball, Gordon Francis | Lance-Corporal | 4343763 | 23 | Tilly-sur-Seulles |
| Clark, Joseph Charles | Private | 5726855 | 23 | Hottot-les-Bagues |
| Clegg, Joseph | Private | 14420474 | 19 | Hottot-les-Bagues |
| Connor, George | Private | 3663782 | 22 | Tilly-sur-Seulles |
| Coombs, Phillip Charles | Lance-Corporal | 6143716 | | Tilly-sur-Seulles |
| Cooper, William Robert | Private | 1223651 | 18 | Tilly-sur-Seulles |
| Cowan, Albert John | Lance-Corporal | 6022209 | 28 | Hottot-les-Bagues |
| Dyke, Charles Arthur James | Lance-Serjeant | 5735740 | 25 | Tilly-sur-Seulles |
| Everitt, Wilfred Henry | Corporal | 6016051 | 23 | Tilly-sur-Seulles |
| Gaskell, Clifford | Private | 14702560 | 18 | Tilly-sur-Seulles |
| Hills, Arthur Edward | Private | 14615848 | 19 | Tilly-sur-Seulles |
| Holland, George Harold | Private | 4923487 | 24 | Tilly-sur-Seulles |
| Hunt, Douglas Haig | Private | 6014833 | 25 | Tilly-sur-Seulles |
| Jordan, Francis | Private | 14643160 | 19 | Tilly-sur-Seulles |
| Joslin, Gordon Alfred | Private | 14702394 | 19 | Tilly-sur-Seulles |
| Lee, John Arthur | Private | 6144676 | 27 | Tilly-sur-Suelles |
| Neal, Ernest William | Private | 6143670 | 23 | Tilly-sur-Seulles |
| Newman, Charles John | Corporal | 6023319 | 29 | Tilly-sur-Seulles |

| | | | | |
|---|---|---|---|---|
| Owers, George Joffre | Private | 5725664 | 29 | Tilly-sur-Seulles |
| Pentecost, Cecil Stanley | Private | 14702344 | 18 | Tilly-sur-Seulles |
| Quaintance, Frederick George | Private | 783397 | 33 | Hottot-les-Bagues |
| Ralph, William Clifford | Private | 4078089 | 22 | Tilly-sur-Seulles |
| Slaney, Charles Austin | Private | 5729173 | 24 | Tilly-sur-Seulles |
| White, William Edward Charles | Private | 5623710 | | Hottot-les-Bagues |
| Wickham, Charles Albert | Private | 6096589 | 28 | Tilly-sur-Seulles |

Private 14702394
Gordon Joslin,
2 Platoon, 'A' Company,
4th Dorsets. Born
26 July 1925 – killed
by machine-gun
fire, 3 August 1944
between La Bigne and
Ondefontaine.

# Other titles published by The History Press

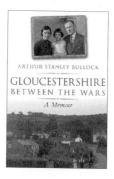

## Gloucestershire Between the Wars: A Memoir
A.S. BULLOCK

One of the most eventful periods in history is vividly and astutely described by Arthur Stanley Bullock in this entertaining memoir. His unique insight comes from having not been in any sense part of the establishment, but instead an ordinary intelligent citizen wit strong sense of moral purpose and an inquisitive mind. Arthur grew up in Longhope in tl Forest of Dean. After his service in the Great War and his struggle to find employment in Birmingham and South Wales, he worked in Dursley. From there he moved to Stroud an set up a business at Port Mills, Brimscombe, just before the onset of the Second World W

978 0 7524 4793 3

## Soldiers of Gloucestershire and North Bristol on the Somme
NICK THORNICROFT

In this informative and moving book, Nick Thornicroft delves into the heart of the Briti Army on the blackest day in its history and gives a vivid portrayal of Gloucestershire and North Bristol soldiers in the heat of battle; these ordinary men in extraordinary circumstances, fighting with incredible bravery for their country's future. Through assiduo research and compassion for his subject, Nick Thornicroft has woven the experiences of Gloucestershire and North Bristol's soldiers into the wider military story, and in doing so brings a human aspect to one of the most inhuman battles in history.

978 0 7524 4325 6

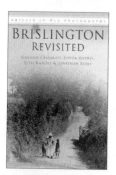

## Brislington Revisited
GRAHAM CRIMMINS, LYNDA HARRIS, BETH KNIGHT & JONATHAN ROWE

In the nineteenth century, Brislington was described as 'the prettiest village in Somerset'. Although it is now a busy suburb of Bristol, it still retains something of its village past, and its history stretches back over 1,000 years. This intriguing book is the second volume illustrating Brislington, containing nearly 200 entirely new images, most of which have nev published before. The faces and buildings, many of which will be recognised by readers today, are representative of their era and will bring back nostalgic memories to locals.

978 0 7542 4555 3

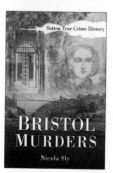

## Bristol Murders
NICOLA SLY

Contained within the pages of *Bristol Murders* are the stories behind some of the most heinous crimes ever committed in Bristol. They include the murder and suicide of a brother and sister in 1842; the tragic death of 10-year-old Mabel Price in 1897; and the suspicious death of sexual deviant Cecil Cornock, which led to his wife Ann being charged with his murder and subsequent acquital in 1946. Nicola Sly's carefully researched, well-illustrated and enthralling text will appeal to anyone interested in the shady side of Bristol's history, and should give much food for thought.

978 0 7509 5048 0

Visit our website and discover thousands of other History Press books.

**www.thehistorypress.co.uk**